W9-CSB-208

CITYPACK

Washington, D.C.

By Bruce Walker and Mary Case

3RD EDITION

Fodor's Travel Publications
New York • Toronto • London • Sydney • Auckland

WWW.FODORS.COM

Contents

About this book

KEY TO SYMBOLS

✚	map reference on the fold-out map accompanying this book (see below)	🚌	nearest bus route
✉	address	🚢	nearest riverboat or ferry stop
☎	telephone number	♿	facilities for visitors with disabilities
🕐	opening times	✋	admission charge
🍴	restaurant or café on premises or nearby	↔	other nearby places of interest
Ⓜ	nearest Metro subway station	❓	tours, lectures, or special events
🚉	nearest railroad station	▶	indicates the page where you will find a fuller description
		ℹ	tourist information

Citypack Washington's six sections cover the six most important aspects of your visit to Washington.

- Washington—the city and its people
- Itineraries, walks and excursions—how to organize your time
- The top 25 sights to visit—arranged from west to east across the city
- Features about different aspects of the city that make it special
- Detailed listings of restaurants, hotels, shops, and nightlife
- Practical information

In addition, text boxes provide fascinating extra facts and snippets, highlights of places to visit and invaluable practical advice.

CROSS-REFERENCES

To help you make the most of your visit, cross-references, indicated by ▶, show you where to find additional information about a place or subject.

MAPS

The fold-out map in the wallet at the back of the book is a comprehensive street plan of Washington. All map references given in the book refer to this map. For example, the White House at 1600 Pennsylvania Avenue has the following information: ✚ F4—indicating the grid square of the map in which the White House will be found.

The downtown maps found on the inside front and back covers of the book itself are for quick reference. They show the top 25 sights, described on pages 24–48, which are clearly plotted by number (❶ – ㉕, not page number) from west to east across the city.

WASHINGTON
life

INTRODUCING WASHINGTON

Pierre L'Enfant

Lasting only a year in the post and never seeing a project completed, the influence of Washington's original designer, Pierre Charles L'Enfant has nevertheless been enormous. Appointed by George Washington in 1791 only to be sacked 12 months later, L'Enfant's vision of a gracious city with airy vistas and wide thoroughfares linking impressive buildings and monuments has been adhered to ever since.

If New York is about money, then Washington is about power, and, just as importantly, access to power. Government is its business—it is the seat of Congress, the House of Representatives and the White House—yet far from being secretive, these institutions freely open their doors to the 20 million tourists who visit each year.

Washington was built from scratch and is the only American city that could invite comparison with Paris and is, in many respects, an outstanding example of 18th-century town planning. The city's layout—its famous broad avenues and wide vistas emphasizing the largely neoclassical architecture of the important federal buildings—still conforms to the concept of its original designer, Pierre L'Enfant. The restriction of buildings to no higher than the Washington Monument (550 feet) has ensured Washington remains skyscraper free.

The impressive Lincoln Memorial

Whether on foot or by public transportation, it is easy to travel around the city. Washington's street grid uses the Capitol as the orienting point. Lettered streets (A to W) run east and west, while numbered streets run north and south. The metro system, which has some of the deepest tunnels in the world, covers all of the metropolitan area with clean and efficient trains and metrobus extends over an even wider area.

Washington is a city of neighborhoods, ranging from the multi-ethnic world of Adams-Morgan to the suburban areas of Woodley Park, Cleveland Park and Rock Creek Park. Washington is a culturally diverse mix of peoples, from African-Americans to Hispanics, Ethiopians to Vietnamese, which creates a vibrant and exciting atmosphere in the neighborhoods. Ethinic festivals offer the chance to explore different cultures.

Washington's foremost attractions are the opportunity to witness government in action and the wealth of superb museums and monuments mostly situated around the two-mile long National Mall and free to all. At its heart is the Smithsonian Institution, the world's largest collection of museums. The city's cultural mix is reflected in its restaurants; you can sample superbly cooked food from a different country every day of the week. A burgeoning theater scene and an excellent selection of art galleries means that Washington offers an exceptional range of cultural as well as political attractions.

Spring at the National Arboretum

7

WASHINGTON IN FIGURES

General
- Number of motor vehicles: 246,000
- Number of radio stations: 47
- Number of broadcast television stations: 19
- Number of movie theaters: 40
- Date became capital: June 10, 1800

Buildings
- Maximum height of any building on Pennsylvania Avenue between the White House and the Capitol: 160 feet
- Oldest and largest U.S. Jesuit college: Georgetown University, founded 1789
- U.S.'s largest Catholic church: National Shrine of the Immaculate Conception
- Oldest surviving structure: the Old Stone House, 3051 M Street NW, begun 1764
- World's tallest masonry structure: Washington Monument, 555 feet
- World's tallest Corinthian columns: National Building Museum, 75 feet

Geography
- Latitude: 38 degrees, 52 minutes
- Longitude: 77 degrees, 00 minutes
- Elevation: 1 foot (near the Potomac River) to 410 feet (Tenley Town in Upper N.W.)
- Area: 68 square miles
- Distance by air to
  New York: 205 miles
  Los Angeles: 2,300 miles
  London: 3,674 miles
  Berlin: 4,181 miles
  Paris: 3,839 miles
- Driving distance to
  Boston: 456 miles
  New York: 233 miles
  Miami: 1,058 miles

People
- Residents first allowed to vote in a presidential election: 1961
- Population (1990): 606,900
- Population (1999): 519,000
- Average per capita annual income: $26,817
- Number of colleges and universities: 10
- Largest employer: the federal government (about 240,000 civilian and military employees)
- Number of federal employees on Capitol Hill: 20,000

WASHINGTON PERSONALITIES

KATHARINE GRAHAM

Currently chairman of the executive committee of The Washington Post Co., Katharine Graham was born in New York in 1917, educated at Vassar and the University of Chicago and became a reporter, later joining the *Washington Post* (owned by her father). She succeeded her husband, Philip L. Graham, as publisher in 1963 after his death. She chose staff wisely, chief among them Benjamin C. Bradlee, who, with Graham's support, firmly established the *Post* as one of the country's leading newspapers with its stories on Watergate and publishing the Pentagon Papers.

HAL GORDON

"I was asking the Lord what I was going to do after I retired when I stumbled over a mound of snow and discovered a nearly frozen man." From that moment, Hal Gordon—retired army officer and business developer—began to touch the lives of homeless men and women with addiction problems. Today, he heads Washington's Community Action Group which houses, feeds, counsels, employs, and encourages the recovery of about 100 people a year. CAG's job development program serves the community by providing dog walkers, trash removers, janitors, house sitters, and the like as participants move back into the mainstream.

SENATOR EDWARD M. KENNEDY

Edward Kennedy has been a Washington figure since 1962, when he was elected to the U.S. Senate to finish the term of his brother, President John F. Kennedy. His political career is rooted in social issues centered on improved health care, education, and civil rights laws. He is held in high regard for his well-thought out and clearly argued welfare policies. His presidential aspirations were blighted by the tragic incident at Chappaquiddick which led to him losing the 1980 Democratic ticket to Jimmy Carter. He continues in political life, and lives in Washington's Kalorama district.

A CHRONOLOGY

1790	President George Washington is authorized by Congress to build a Federal City.
1791	Washington hires Pierre Charles L'Enfant to design a city on the banks of the Potomac River, siting, according to legend, the U.S. Capitol in the exact center of the 13 original states.
1800	President Adams occupies the unfinished White House, and Congress meets in the Capitol, also unfinished. Population now 3,000.
1812	United States declares war on Britain.
1814	The British sack Washington, burning many public buildings, including the White House and the Capitol. Original Library of Congress burned.
1844	Samuel F. B. Morse transmits the first telegraph message from the Capitol to Baltimore, MD.
1846	Congress accepts James Smithson's bequest and establishes the Smithsonian Institution.
1850	The slave trade abolished in the District.
1863	Lincoln issues the Emancipation Proclamation, freeing the nation's slaves. This begins an influx of former slaves to the nation's capital.
1867	Howard University is chartered by Congress to educate blacks.
1876	The nation's centennial is celebrated with a fair in Philadelphia. Fifty-six train cars are filled with material to be donated to the Smithsonian. The District's population is about 140,000.
1901	President McKinley authorizes the McMillan Commission to oversee the city's beautification.
1908	Trains are diverted to the new Union Station, which includes a Presidential Waiting Room.
1917	The U.S. enters World War I; the population reaches 400,000 as the city enjoys a boom.

1941	The U.S. enters World War II.
1958	The East Front extension of the Capitol begins, adding 102 offices.
1961	President John F. Kennedy plans the renovation of Pennsylvania Avenue. Residents are given the right to vote in presidential elections.
1963	Martin Luther King, Jr., delivers his "I Have a Dream" speech from the Lincoln Memorial.
1968	King delivers his last sermon at Washington National Cathedral. His shooting in Memphis five days later sparks riots; some areas are burned.
1968–73	Demonstrations against the Vietnam War on the National Mall.
1974	The Watergate Hotel becomes infamous as the site of the bungled Republican robbery attempt on Democratic headquarters. President Richard Nixon resigns as a result of the ensuing cover-up.
1976	Many Bicentennial celebrations are focused on Washington. The Metrorail opens.
1981	President Ronald Reagan is shot outside his car at the Washington Hilton.
1984	The renovated Old Post Office reopens and revives this section of Pennsylvania Avenue.
1988	Opening of the restored Union Station.
1990	Washington National Cathedral is completed after 73 years. Mayor Sharon Pratt Dixon Kelly is the first black woman to head a major U.S. city.
1993	The U.S. Holocaust Memorial Museum opens.
1997	Washington National Airport expansion complete; MCI sports arena opens, Downtown.
1999	President Clinton impeached by Congress in the midst of the strongest U.S. economy ever.

PEOPLE & EVENTS FROM HISTORY

"Duke" Ellington

Edward Kennedy Ellington, born in 1899, grew up in Washington (► 50). Often called the most influential American composer, Ellington concerned himself with jazz composition and musical form, as distinct from improvization, writing, and arranging. He also sustained and supported an orchestra to perform his incomparable music. Upon his death in 1974, the Duke Ellington School for the Arts was established in his honor.

FREDERICK LAW OLMSTED, SR.

Born in 1822 in Hartford, CT, the nation's first landscape architect began work on the grounds of the U.S. Capitol in 1874, creating the west front's vast sweep of lawn and trees. His many achievements include New York's Central Park and Boston's Emerald Necklace; the Olmsted Walk at the National Zoological Park reveals his genius for creating naturalistic environments. In 1866 he designed the grounds of Gallaudet University, the country's first university for people with hearing impairments. At his insistence, Congress passed legislation to safeguard Rock Creek area as the park we enjoy today. He died in 1903.

MARY McLEOD BETHUNE

Daughter of slaves, presidential adviser, energetic teacher, advocate for young people, and champion of human rights, Mary McLeod Bethune (1875–1955) founded the National Council of Negro Women and Daytona Normal and Industrial Institute for Negro Girls (now Bethune-Cookman College). Her achievements were commemorated in 1974 with the dedication of Robert Berk's Bethune Memorial in Lincoln Park. In the same year, Thomas Ball's bronze sculpture, *Emancipation*, in Lincoln Park since 1876, was resited opposite her memorial as a tribute to Bethune's work for African-American women and children. Her home houses the Bethune Museum and Archives (► 54).

A DREAM OF EQUALITY

On August 28, 1963, Martin Luther King, Jr., delivered his vision of racial harmony and equality from the steps of the Lincoln Memorial to a crowd of 200,000. Born in 1929, King set up the first black ministry in Alabama in 1955 and became the figurehead of a non-violent civil rights movement fighting to end segregation and discrimination. His "I Have a Dream" speech was the culmination of a march on Washington by blacks and whites calling for reform, and he was awarded the Nobel Peace Prize in 1964. King was assassinated in 1968.

WASHINGTON
how to organize your time

ITINERARIES

Walking the length of the grassy Mall from the Capitol (► 43) to the Lincoln Memorial (► 26) can be exhilarating, even on hot summer days. The scale of the federal buildings and their placement in formal landscapes provide powerful, carefully controlled vistas.

ITINERARY ONE	**CAPITOL HILL & GEORGETOWN**
Morning	Visit the Supreme Court (► 45), Capitol (► 43), and Library of Congress (► 46).
Lunch	Enjoy the view and lunch in the Library of Congress's Madison Building cafeteria.
Afternoon	Walk down the hill to the Botanic Gardens (► 42) or the National Air and Space Museum (► 41).
Evening	If you are on The Hill (as Capitol Hill is known), check the light in the cupola. If it's shining, Congress is working late and the building will be open, even to tourists. Walk right in! Take a cab to Washington Harbor (► 18), a dining and entertainment complex with boardwalk, restaurants, offices, and apartments.
ITINERARY TWO	**ART, ARCHIVES, AIR & SPACE**
Morning	Visit the National Archives (► 39) and National Gallery of Art (► 40).
Lunch	The National Gallery of Art has a couple of options.
Afternoon	Choose from the National Air and Space Museum (► 41) or National Museum of Natural History or, to see more art, try the Smithsonian museums clustered near the Castle (► 36): the Hirshhorn Museum and Sculpture Garden, the National Museum of African Art, the Sackler and the Freer Galleries.
Evening	At the John F. Kennedy Center (► 25), have a pre-theater dinner and see a show.

ITINERARY THREE	AROUND THE TIDAL BASIN
Morning	Visit the U.S. Holocaust Memorial Museum (➤ 33).
Lunch	Have a bite to eat at the Holocaust Museum's Kosher Cafeteria.
Afternoon	Visit the Bureau of Engraving and Printing (➤ 35); then stroll around the Tidal Basin and visit the Jefferson Memorial (➤ 32), the Franklin Delano Roosevelt Memorial (➤ 57), and finally the Lincoln Memorial (➤ 26).
Evening	Take a cab to Union Station (➤ 44) for dinner, shopping, or a movie.
ITINERARY FOUR	WHITE HOUSE & DUPONT CIRCLE
Morning	Start at the White House Information Center (➤ 30), and after a tour of 1600 Pennsylvania Avenue, visit the FBI building (➤ 37).
Lunch	Take the Metro to Dupont Circle to lunch at one of the many Connecticut Avenue restaurants.
Afternoon	Explore the stores and small museums, including the modern art paintings at the Phillips Collection (➤ 27), in and around Dupont Circle (➤ 17). People-watch in a sidewalk café then browse in the bookstores—some open all night.
Evening	Have dinner in Adams-Morgan (➤ 18) and dance the night away.

Dupont Circle café

WALKS

THE SIGHTS

INFORMATION

Time 2¾ hours
Distance 1½ miles
Start point U.S. Capitol
🚇 J5
🚊 Capitol South
End point White House
🚇 F4
🚊 McPherson Square

Freedom Plaza

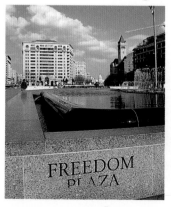

FREEDOM
PLAZA

THE CAPITOL TO THE WHITE HOUSE

Immediately following the Inauguration, the president and his entourage descend the west face of the Capitol and proceed, in cars or sometimes on foot, up Pennsylvania Avenue to the White House. This walk takes the same route.

Begin on the west steps of the Capitol building, overlooking the wide, grassy swath of the National Mall. The view takes in the memorial core of Washington, from the Botanic Gardens and federal office buildings on the left along Maryland Avenue, to the Washington Monument and Lincoln Memorial directly ahead, to the domes of the National Museum of Natural History and National Gallery of Art, and the Federal Triangle complex on the right.

Follow Pennsylvania Avenue, passing or exploring the National Gallery of Art, the Canadian Embassy, the National Archives, and the Navy Memorial. Turn right onto the thriving art corridor of 7th Street up to Chinatown Metro and the golden Friendship Arch of Washington's Asian community. Go west along G Street and turn left onto 10th Street past Ford's Theater, where Abraham Lincoln was fatally wounded on April 14, 1865. The main FBI building is on the left.

Turn right onto Pennsylvania Avenue. The fanciful granite 'old tooth' clock tower of the Old Post Office stands out amid its surroundings and offers an unsurpassed city view. Farther up Pennsylvania is Freedom Plaza, with its incised stone map of L'Enfant's city plan, and Pershing Park, serving as a front yard to the Willard Hotel and to the White House Information Center. Turn right onto 15th Street, past the 1836 Treasury Building, which appears on the $10 bill, and take a left onto Pennsylvania Avenue in front of the White House.

COSMOPOLITAN WASHINGTON

Dupont Circle is the heart of chic, single Washington and a focus of gay culture. Clubs, restaurants, bookstores, coffee shops, and boutiques line Connecticut Avenue and P Street on both sides of the Circle. Distinctive small museums and art galleries, embassies, and important architecture are on the route.

Begin at Dupont Circle Metro's Q Street exit. Go east on Q to 1700, past Thomas F. Schneider's town houses (1889–92). The steel-framed Cairo Apartments (1894) at 1615 Q prompted Congress to introduce height restrictions. Turn south onto 17th Street and right onto Church Street. The altar and back wall of an early episcopal church, destroyed by arson in 1970, frame an inviting pocket park. Turn left onto 18th and right onto P to the Italianate Patterson House (1901–03). Hartman-Cox's 1970 Euram Building at 21 Dupont Circle demonstrates that creativity can flourish despite Washington's strict building codes. Rest a moment in the courtyard.

Turn left onto New Hampshire Avenue to 1307, the Historical Society of Washington. Take a right onto 20th, then a left onto Massachusetts. On the left is the Walsh Mansion, purchased by Indonesia in 1951 for one-tenth of the $3,000,000 it cost to build in 1903. At 1600 21st Street is the Phillips Collection, America's first modern art museum. Continue to 2118 Massachusetts Avenue and pass the walled courtyard of Anderson House (1902–5). In the 2200 block and Sheridan Circle architecturally diverse embassies line the avenue.

Turn right onto S Street, stopping at Woodrow Wilson House and the Textile Museum. Walk down the delightful Decatur Terrace Steps. Turn left onto Decatur Place, left onto Florida Avenue and continue to Connecticut Avenue and onto Dupont Circle Metro.

Italian eating, Dupont Circle

THE SIGHTS

- Schneider's terraced houses
- The Cairo Apartment Building
- Patterson House
- Euram Building
- Historical Society of Washington (➤ 54)
- Walsh Mansion
- Phillips Collection (➤ 27)
- Anderson House
- Sheridan Circle
- Embassies of Togo, Sudan, Greece, Egypt, Kenya, Philippines
- Woodrow Wilson House
- Textile Museum
- Decatur Terrace Steps

INFORMATION

Time 1½ hours

Distance 2½ miles

Start and end point Dupont Circle

➕ F3

🚇 Dupont Circle

EVENING STROLLS

INFORMATION

Adams-Morgan
Distance 1¹/₂ miles
Time 3 hours
Start point 18th Street at
Columbia Road
⊞ F2
🚇 Dupont Circle
End point Dupont Circle Metro
⊞ F3

Georgetown
Distance 1¹/₂ miles
Time 2 hours
Start and end points
Washington Harbor, 3000 K
Street NW
Best reached by cab
⊞ E4

Georgetown

ADAMS-MORGAN

Adams-Morgan takes its name from its elementary schools—historically white "Adams" and historically African-American "Morgan". Each new wave of immigrants adds to the neighborhood's diverse mix. From 18th Street NW at Columbia Road walk two or three blocks in any direction, and you'll find sidewalk cafés, stores, galleries, and clubs. You can eat Mexican, Indian, Ethiopian, French, Caribbean, or Argentinian among others, and some restaurants turn into lively dance clubs after 11PM. Afterwards, walk south to Dupont Circle Metro.

GEORGETOWN

Take a cab to exuberant Washington Harbor, 3000 K Street NW. Have a meal here or just enjoy the fountains, outdoor sculpture, and boardwalk along the Potomac River. Walk up 30th Street NW, stopping at the Chesapeake and Ohio Canal; you can walk, jog, or bike for miles along its towpath. Staying on 30th Street NW, walk a block farther up the hill to M Street, lined with small restaurants and boutiques. Go left two blocks to Wisconsin Avenue and the heart of Georgetown. Shops here sell everything, from hip outfits for the X-Generation to tailored clothing for the well-to-do residents of Georgetown's 18th-century town houses.

Organized Sightseeing

GRAY LINE TOURS

Gray Line buses take in major Washington sites, including Embassy Row and travel out-of-town to Mount Vernon and Alexandria.

➕ J4 ✉ Gray Line terminal, Union Station; also 5500 Tuxedo Road, Tuxedo, MD 20781 ☎ 301/386–8300, 800/862–1400, extension 320 🕐 Tours all year 🚇 Union Station 💰 Prices vary with tour

Old Town Trolley Tour

DISCOVERY STORE WALK

This 1–1½ hour walk takes you through historic Chinatown and Washington's original residential and commercial areas.

➕ H4 ✉ 700 G Street NW ☎ 202/639–0908 🕐 Sat, Sun 1:30 🚇 Gallery Place/Chinatown 💰 Moderate, children under five go free

NATIONAL PARK SERVICE

The National Park Service produces a brochure on the Black History National Recreation Trail.

➕ G6 ✉ 1100 Ohio Drive SW ☎ 202/619–7222 💰 Free

OLD TOWN TROLLEY TOURS

In addition to the memorial core, you'll visit Georgetown, the National Zoo, and Washington Cathedral. The trolleys run every half-hour and you can board them at any of their stops. Shorter evening tours are available.

☎ 301/985–3021, 800/868–7482 🕐 Tours all year 💰 Moderate, children under three ride free

THE SMITHSONIAN ASSOCIATES

Smithsonian walking and bus tours through area neighborhoods are often topical—African-American life, *beaux-arts* architecture, public gardens, artists' studios.

➕ G5 ✉ The Castle, Jefferson Drive at 10th Street SW ☎ 202/357–2700 💰 Prices vary with tour

TOURMOBILE

You can step on and off Tourmobiles at any of their stops near most of the sites in this guide.

☎ 202/554–7950, 202/554–5100 🕐 Tours all year ♿ Wheelchair-equipped vans available 💰 Moderate

Personal guides

For tour guides for individuals or groups, in almost any language, try:

A Tour de Force

✉ Box 2782, Washington, DC 20013

☎ 703/525–2948

Guide Service of Washington

✉ 733 15th Street Suite 1040, Washington, DC 20005

☎ 202/628–2842

Anthony Pitch

Walking tours through historic Georgetown, Victorian Adams-Morgan, Lafayette Square and the White House

✉ 9009 Paddock Lane, Potomac, MD 20854

☎ 301/251–1765

Sonny Odem

This is the person to call if photography is your thing. You'll come home with the best travel photographs you've ever taken

✉ 2504-B Walter Reed Drive, Arlington, VA 22206

☎ 703/379–1633.

EXCURSIONS

INFORMATION

Old Town Alexandria
Distance 6 miles
Journey time 20 minutes by car
🚇 King Street Station, then
board Dash bus AT2 or AT5
eastbound.
By car Take the 14th
Street Bridge (toward
National Airport); then
George Washington Parkway
to King Street.
By bike Start at the Lincoln
Memorial and cross Memorial
Bridge heading south 5.6
miles to Alexandria.
🛈 Ramsay House Visitors
Center ✉ 221 King Street
☎ 703/838–4200
🕐 Daily 9–5

Mount Vernon
Distance 17 miles
Journey time 40 minutes by car
☎ 703/780–2000
🕐 Daily 9–5
🚌 Tourmobile and Gray Line
Tours make daily trips,
Mar–Oct
By car 14th Street Bridge
(toward National Airport),
then south on George
Washington Memorial
Parkway.
By bike Start at the Lincoln
Memorial and cross Memorial
Bridge heading south
🚢 *Potomac Spirit* from Pier 4,
6th and Water Streets SW
☎ 202/554–8000
💰 Expensive

OLD TOWN ALEXANDRIA

This Virginia community is a window onto a sophisticated version of small-town America with its colonial seaport architecture and traditions. Old Town, which is easily covered on foot, includes hundreds of colonial buildings, many of them open to the public. The Torpedo Factory Arts Center houses Historic Alexandria, which conducts archeological research in the area, and dozens of artisans are often on hand to discuss the exhibits as well as their own work. Start at the Ramsay House Visitors Center, where you can get tickets to numerous historic properties, parking permits, walking guides, and restaurant and shopping recommendations.

MOUNT VERNON

George Washington's ancestral Virginia estate is the nation's second most-visited historic house after the White House. Its Ladies Association, formed in 1853 to preserve the estate, is credited with starting the historic preservation movement in the United States. The mansion overlooks the Potomac River and is built of yellow pine painted to resemble stone. The ornate interior is furnished with fine arts and memorabilia from the last years of Washington's life. The outbuildings re-create the spaces of a self-sufficient 18th-century farm, including the smokehouse and laundry, outside kitchen and slave quarters. On the river side, don't miss the view of the Potomac, and George and Martha Washington's tomb.

*Old Town
Alexandria*

FREDERICKSBURG

The 40-block National Historic District in this charming Virginia town comprises the house George Washington bought his mother, a 1752 plantation, James Monroe's law offices, an early apothecary shop, and the Georgian Chatham Manor, overlooking the Rappahannock River. Many Civil War battles were waged in and around town, and you can hike in the battlefields and in nearby wilderness parks. Antiques and rare-book stores, and art galleries line the streets. Start at the well-marked Visitors Center, which dispenses maps and advice.

SOLOMONS

This part of Maryland south of Washington retains its rural character and is worth an excursion, though you'll need a car. The Calvert Marine Museum explores the Chesapeake Bay and its commercial fishing, maritime history, and estuarine biology. On the town's pleasant three-block river walk you will encounter several species of duck, plus historic churches, quaint bed and breakfast establishments, modern hotels, fishing spots, seafood restaurants, and a well-maintained wetlands park and beach. The infor-mation center can give you travel tips. This is a great place to bike for an afternoon or just settle in on one of the wide porches and watch the sailboats in the bay.

George Washington's estate, Mount Vernon

INFORMATION

Fredericksburg
Distance 50 miles
Journey time 1–2 hours by car
🚆 Amtrak from Union Station. About 1¼ hours' travel time.
  By car south on I-95 to exit 130A and follow signs to the Visitors Center
🛈 706 Caroline Street
  Fredericksburg, VA 22401
  ☎ 540/373–1776 or 800/678–4748
  🕐 Daily 9–5

Solomons
Distance 60 miles
Journey time 1–2 hours
  By car Pennsylvania Avenue South, which turns into Route 4. Follow the signs for Calvert Marine Museum and Solomons Island
🛈 Route 2, Solomons
  ☎ 410/326–6027
  🕐 Jun–Oct: daily 9–5.
  Nov–May: Thu–Sat 9–5

21

WHAT'S ON

January	*Washington Antiques Show* ☎ 202/234–0700. Congress returns the first week.
February	*Martin Luther King, Jr. Birthday Observation* ☎ 202/727–1186. *Lincoln's Birthday* ☎ 202/619–7275. *Chinese New Year's Parade* ☎ 202/638–1041.
March	*St. Patrick's Day Festival* ☎ 202/879–1717. *Organist's Bach Marathon* ☎ 202/363–2202. *Smithsonian Kite Flying Festival* ☎ 202/357–2700.
April	*National Cherry Blossom Festival* ☎ 202/728–1137. *White House Spring Garden Tour* ☎ 202/456–7041.
May	*Washington National Cathedral Flower Mart* ☎ 202/537–6200. *Mother's Day: Capitol Hill Restoration Society House Tour* ☎ 202/543–0425.
June	*Big Band Concert Series* ☎ 202/619–7222.
July	*Smithsonian Festival of American Folklife* ☎ 202/357–2700. *Independence Day* (Jul 4) ☎ 202/619–7222.
August	Everybody's at the beach.
September	*National Symphony Orchestra Labor Day Concert* ☎ 202/467–4600. *Adams-Morgan Day* ☎ 202/332–3292. *Black Family Reunion* ☎ 202/383–9104.
October	*Washington International Horse Show* ☎ 301/840–0281. *Marine Corps Marathon* ☎ 703/690–3431. *Taste of D.C. Festival* ☎ 202/724–5430.
November	*Veterans' Day Activities* ☎ 202/475–0843.
December	*People's Christmas Tree Lighting* ☎ 202/224–3069.

WASHINGTON's
top 25 sights

The sights are shown on the maps on the inside front cover and inside back cover, numbered **1–25** *from west to east across the city*

ARLINGTON NATIONAL CEMETERY

HIGHLIGHTS

- Kennedy graves
- Tomb of the Unknowns
- Custis-Lee Mansion
- L'Enfant's grave
- U.S.S. Marine Memorial
- Shuttle *Challenger*
- Astronauts Memorial
- Changing of the Guard at the Tomb of the Unknowns

INFORMATION

- C6–D7
- ANC, Arlington, VA 22211
- 703/607–8052
- Apr–Sep: daily 8–7.
  Oct–Mar: daily 8–5
- Arlington Cemetery
- Tourmobile
- Excellent. Visitors with disabilities may board Tourmobile Shuttles or obtain driving permit at the Visitors Center
- Free
- Lincoln Memorial (➤ 26), Vietnam Veterans Memorial (➤ 28), Francis Scott Key Bridge (➤ 60)
- Narrated Tourmobile Shuttle, every 20 minutes. Changing of the Guard: Apr–Sep daily on the half hour; Oct–Mar daily on the hour. Parking available at the cemetery

The official national cemetery since 1883, Arlington famously contains the most visited gravesite in the country, that of John F. Kennedy. Rows of simple white headstones commemorate with dignity America's war dead, and national heroes.

Lest we forget The first burial at the Tomb of the Unknowns occurred on November 11, 1921. This World War I soldier was joined in 1958 by honored dead from World War II and Korea and, for 15 years beginning in 1984, by a Vietnam veteran. In 1999, new DNA techniques facilitated the identification of the Vietnam veteran, who was subsequently moved by his family. Sentries perform with great precision and skill a regular Changing of the Guard ceremony.

White markers and a flame Under an eternal flame, John F. Kennedy lies next to his wife, Jacqueline Bouvier Kennedy Onassis, and two of his children who died in infancy. Nearby lies his brother, Robert Kennedy, slain in 1968, whose grave is marked by a simple white cross and a fountain. Above the Kennedy graves stands the Greek Revival Custis-Lee Mansion (also known as Arlington House), built between 1802 and 1817 by George Washington Parke Custis, grandson of Martha and step-grandson of George Washington. Just off the west corner of the house lies the grave of Pierre L'Enfant, now overlooking for eternity the Federal City that he designed in the face of difficulties that left him penniless and embittered. Throughout the 612-acre cemetery, row upon row of simple white markers stand erect like the soldiers once did themselves. Memorials commemorate a particular event or group of people. In 1997, a memorial was dedicated to women who lost their lives in military service.

JOHN F. KENNEDY CENTER

With five theaters of differing sizes, this national cultural center covers eight acres and is the jewel in the crown of the city's arts venues. A stroll on the roof terrace provides a stunning 360-degree view of Washington and the Potomac River.

The seat of the arts   Opened in 1971, Edward Durrell Stone's simple white marble box overlooks the Potomac River next to the Watergate complex, infamous for the 1972 bungled attempt to bug the Democratic National Committee which eventually led to President Richard Nixon's resignation. When the Kennedy Center opened, the Washington performing arts scene took a great leap forward; the opera house and concert hall especially have splendid acoustics.

Hall of States   The building is sheathed in 3,700 tons of white Carrara marble, a gift from Italy. The Grand Foyer, 630 feet long and 60 feet high, blazes from the light of 18 Orrefors crystal chandeliers, donated by Sweden and reflected in 60-foot-high mirrors, a gift from Belgium. Overlooking theatergoers is a bust of John F. Kennedy by Robert Berks, who also designed the Albert Einstein Memorial. The expansive lobby, called the Hall of States, displays state flags arranged in the order in which the states were admitted to the Union. One end of the hall is devoted to the Millennium Stage where performances are given in the evening. The building also accommodates two stage theaters, a movie theater, a theater lab, and the Performing Arts Library of the Library of Congress. Many of these can be seen on a tour of the building or at intermission during a performance.

HIGHLIGHTS

- Hall of States
- View from the roof terrace
- Henri Matisse tapestries, a gift from France

INFORMATION

- E4–E5
- New Hampshire Avenue at Rock Creek Parkway NW
- 202/467–4600; 800/444–1324
- Daily for tours and performances as scheduled
- Encore Café; Roof Terrace Restaurant: call 202/416–8555 for hours
- Foggy Bottom. Free bus shuttle service every 15 minutes 5–11:45PM
- Excellent
- Free tours; performance ticket prices vary
- Georgetown (▶ 18), Lincoln Memorial (▶ 26)
- Free one-hour tours between 10AM and 1PM. Free Millennium Stage performance daily at 6PM

Matisse tapestry

3

LINCOLN MEMORIAL

HIGHLIGHTS

- Daniel Chester French's *Lincoln*
- Inscription of Lincoln's 1863 Gettysburg Address and Second Inaugural Address
- Underground exhibit on First Amendment rights
- Reflecting pool
- View

INFORMATION

- E5
- The Mall at 23rd Street NW
- 202/426–6841
- 24 hours; staffed 8AM–midnight
- Foggy Bottom
- Excellent
- Free
- Vietnam Veterans Memorial (➤ 28), Jefferson Memorial (➤ 32), Korean War Memorial (➤ 57)
- Tours available upon request

So powerful and somber is this memorial that you can easily imagine Lincoln rising up and resuming his epic struggles. The view from the steps at sunset is one of the city's most romantic, with the Washington Monument reflected in the rectangular pool at its base.

Tribute John Wilkes Booth shot Abraham Lincoln in Ford's Theater on April 14, 1865. Lincoln died the next day. Four decades passed before congressional and public support reached a consensus on the design and siting of a monument to this well-loved president. Work began on the memorial on the eve of World War I and continued until 1922, when Henry Bacon's Greek temple was dedicated.

History in stone The 36 columns symbolize the 36 states in the Union when Lincoln died. The names of the 48 states in the Union, at the time of the monument's dedication, are inscribed above the parapet's crowning frieze. The 8-ton, 19-foot marble statue by Daniel Chester French captures a contemplative Lincoln. The monument's construction is chronicled in a small museum on the lower level. Lincoln's Gettysburg Address and his Second Inaugural Address are inscribed on the south and north walls. It was here on the steps, a century after Lincoln emancipated the slaves, that Martin Luther King, Jr., delivered his famous "I Have a Dream" speech before a crowd of 200,000 people.

The colonnaded facade of the Lincoln Memorial

26

4

PHILLIPS COLLECTION

Washington's distinguished museums include the first permanent modern art museum in the United States, the Phillips Collection. The collection comprises more than 25,000 works, of which between 250 and 300 are on exhibit at any one time in this intimate gallery.

Unique collection In 1921 Duncan Phillips opened two gallery rooms in his Georgian Revival mansion as a memorial to his father and brother. In the same year he married painter Marjorie Acker. Together they assembled an unparalleled collection of French Impressionists—including Auguste Renoir's *Luncheon of the Boating Party*, acquired in 1923 for the then record price of $125,000—Post-Impressionists, Cubists, 17th- and 18th-century masters, and American Modernists. They avoided the ordinary and sought out paintings that glowed with an artist's unique vision; their unerring eye has given the collection a special quality. The enlarged but still intimate Goh annex, which opened in 1989, provides additional space for traveling exhibitions and for exhibitions of the permanent collection, which change periodically.

Masterpieces The playful Swiss painter Paul Klee is well represented here, as is the master of brilliant domestic images, Pierre Bonnard. Americans Arthur Dove, Georgia O'Keeffe, and Mark Rothko coexist peacefully alongside Pablo Picasso, Claude Monet, and Edgar Degas. The Music Room on the first floor, with its oak paneling and wainscoting, displays works by one of Phillips's favorite artists, Cubist Georges Braque. The paintings are hung throughout the house, and art students, who serve as wardens, are always willing to discuss works in detail.

HIGHLIGHTS

- *Luncheon of the Boating Party*, Renoir
- *The Way to the Citadel*, Paul Klee
- *Repentant Peter*, El Greco
- *Entrance to the Public Garden at Arles*, Van Gogh
- *Dancers at the Bar*, Degas
- American Modernists
- *The Terrace*, Pierre Bonnard

INFORMATION

- ✛ F3
- ✉ 1600–1612 21st Street NW
- ☎ 202/387-2151
- ◷ Tue–Sat 10–5 (Thu 5–9); Sun 12–7
- 🍴 Café
- Ⓜ Dupont Circle
- ♿ Excellent
- 💵 Moderate Sat, Sun; contributions Mon–Fri
- ↔ John F. Kennedy Center (► 25), National Geographic Society (► 29)
- ❓ Tours Wed and Sat 2PM. Concerts in the Music Room Sep–May: Sun 5PM

Luncheon of the Boating Party *by Pierre Auguste Renoir (1881)*

27

5

VIETNAM VETERANS MEMORIAL

HIGHLIGHTS

- Inscribed names
- Frederick Hart's sculptural group
- Glenna Goodacre's sculptural group
- The city reflected in the polished stone

INFORMATION

- E5
- Near Constitution Avenue between 21st and 22nd Streets, NW
- 202/634–1568
- 24 hours; staffed 8AM–midnight
- Foggy Bottom
- Excellent
- Free
- Presidents' Monuments (➤ 26, 31, 32); Einstein Memorial (➤ 56); Korean War Memorial (➤ 57)
- Rangers available to assist in locating names and to provide paper and graphite suitable for taking a rubbing of the names

Names on the Wall

This starkly simple sculpture has been called the most moving memorial in Washington, and on most days there is an almost constant procession of quiet visitors moving down into what one veteran called the "black gash of shame."

Simple reminder Yale University student Maya Ying Lin was only 21 when she won the national design competition with a memorial that is simplicity itself: two triangular black granite walls, each 246 feet 8 inches long, set at a 125-degree angle and pointing towards the Washington Monument and Lincoln Memorial. At the memorial's apex, the walls rise to 10 feet and seem to overpower those who stand beneath them. The names of heroes who made the ultimate sacrifice for their country are placed chronologically: between 1959 and 1975, more than 58,000 were killed or reported missing in action. It was the longest armed war in American history.

A place to reflect The polished surface reflects sky, trees, nearby monuments, and the faces of visitors searching for the names of fathers, sons, and loved ones. Each day National Park Service Rangers collect mementoes left near soldier's names: letters, uniforms, military emblems, photographs. These tokens receive the care of museum acquisitions and are held by the National Park Service in perpetuity as part of the history of the nation. Initially, some veterans thought the Wall insufficient to represent them. So in 1984 Frederick Hart's slightly larger-than-life sculpture of three soldiers was dedicated, sited at one of the entrances to the Wall. The Vietnam Women's Memorial, a figural sculpture by Glenna Goodacre, was dedicated nearby on Veterans' Day in 1993.

NATIONAL GEOGRAPHIC SOCIETY

Gilbert Hovey Grosvenor, who founded the yellow-bordered National Geographic magazine in 1888, brought geography alive for his readers by his use of stunning photography, and the Society continues this tradition of breathing life into a subject in its splendid exhibits.

Architectural history Since 1888, the Society has increased and diffused geographic knowledge as directed by its charter, in part via the familiar yellow monthly *National Geographic* magazine. The National Geo buildings—1902 *beaux-arts* original, 1964 Edward Durrell Stone's dominant ten-story tower, and the 1984 Skidmore, Owings and Merrill angular terraced ziggurat—create an enclave of 20th-century American architecture.

Living world Explorers Hall is on the first floor of the society's glass-and-marble building which was designed by Kennedy Center architect Edward Durrell Stone. *Geographica*, a high-tech, celebratory exhibit installed for the magazine's centennial in 1988, lets you touch a tornado, explore a Martian landscape, test your knowledge of early human development, investigate undersea archeology, and learn trivia about space. Here, too, is the world's largest freestanding globe, 11 feet tall and 34 feet in circumference, which shows earth at a scale of 1 inch to 60 miles. There are also short films, and an interactive amphitheater called Earth Station One, that simulates orbital flight and looks at earth from out in space. Stunning images taken by the Society's legendary photographers enhance every exhibition. The gift shop sells Society maps, books, videos, and CD-ROMs.

HIGHLIGHTS

- World's largest freestanding globe
- Touch a tornado
- Earth Station One
- Holographic images
- Model of Jacques Cousteau's diving saucer
- Moon rock

INFORMATION

- F3
- 17th and M Streets NW
- 202/857–7588
- Mon–Sat 9–5; Sun 10–5
- Dupont Circle, Farragut North
- Excellent
- Free. Tue noon: free showings of National Geographic specials in the T.V. room
- Dupont Circle (➤ 17)

THE WHITE HOUSE

HIGHLIGHTS

- *Abraham Lincoln*, G. P. A. Healy
- Jacqueline Kennedy Rose Garden
- French and English gilded silver
- East Room
- *George Washington*, Gilbert Stuart

INFORMATION

- F4
- 1600 Pennsylvania Avenue
- 202/456–7041
- Tue–Sat 10–noon
- McPherson Square, Metro Center
- Excellent
- Free
- Washington Monument (▶ 31)
- For free timed tickets and historical exhibits, go to the White House Visitors Center, 15th and E Streets NW, Daily 7:30–4. During busy seasons, the line begins to form at 6AM. American citizens can contact their congressmen for advance tickets

In the city's oldest public building, virtually every desk, every sterling tea service, every silver platter, decanter, painting, and floor covering in the house intertwines with the historic events of the American democracy.

History Despite the fact that Thomas Jefferson thought James Hogan's original design "big enough for two emperors, one Pope, and the grand Lama" when he became the second occupant of 1600 Pennsylvania Avenue in 1801, the third President built additional wings to house domestic quarters for the president and offices. Today the White House looks modest, flanked as it is by the U.S. Treasury, the largest Greek Revival building in the world, and the ten-acre Old Executive Office Building. The British burned the White House in 1814, and the rebuilding that followed was only one of several renovations conducted over the years.

Works of art The president's house holds an impressive display of decorative arts from the Sheraton, French and American Empire, Queen Anne, and Federal periods. There are carved Carrara marble mantels, Bohemian cut-glass chandeliers, Turkish Hereke carpets, and elaborate plasterwork throughout, as well as the gardens. The exact tour may vary depending on official functions, but usually open are the ceremonial East Room, with Gilbert Stuart's 1797 portrait of George Washington, the Vermeil Room containing 17th- to early 20th-century French and English gilded silver (vermeil), the small drawing-room known as the Green Room, the neo-classical State Dining Room where George P. A. Healy's Abraham Lincoln portrait hangs, and the Blue and Red Rooms, known for their superb French Empire furnishings.

WASHINGTON MONUMENT

An icon of Washington life, this monolith is the world's tallest masonry structure. The 70-second ride to the pinnacle is rewarded by a marvellous perspective right across the District, as well as over Maryland, and Virginia.

Money The Washington Monument, which punctuates the axis of the White House and Jefferson Memorial, and the U.S. Congress and Lincoln Memorial, perfectly exemplifies how government projects can go awry. A 1783 Congressional resolution called for an equestrian statue to honor George Washington for his heroic leadership during the American Revolution. Nothing happened until 1836, when private citizens formed the Washington National Monument Society and solicited one dollar from every living American. When they had raised $28,000, the group laid the cornerstone to Robert Mills's design in 1848. The Civil War interrupted work on the obelisk; construction did not resume until 1876, sparked by the national fervor surrounding the centennial of the American Revolution. Note how the color of the marble changes 150 feet from the ground.

View The monument comprises 555 feet, 5½ inches of marble obelisk, with views from the top over most of the District and parts of Maryland and Virginia: look for the Tidal Basin, the Jefferson and Lincoln memorials, the White House, the U.S. Capitol, the Library of Congress, and the Smithsonian Institution. If you take the weekend guided walk down the monument's 898 steps you will see the commemorative plaques donated during building by states, masonic lodges, church groups, and foreign countries. The exhibit in the monument's base recounts the recent renovation.

HIGHLIGHTS

- Views from the top
- Exhibit in base

INFORMATION

- F5–G5
- The Mall at 15th Street NW
- 202/426–6840
- Apr–Labor Day: daily 8AM–midnight. Labor Day–Mar: daily 9–5.
- Smithsonian
- Excellent
- Free
- Timed tickets distributed daily at 8:30AM and through Ticketmaster ☎ 301/808–2405. Guided tours Sat, Sun 10, 2. Lines are shorter at night

The 555-foot obelisk

JEFFERSON MEMORIAL

HIGHLIGHTS

- Jefferson bronze
- Inscribed Declaration of Independence
- Jefferson's statement on the separation of church and state
- Cherry blossoms in April

INFORMATION

- ✚ F6
- ✉ Tidal Basin, south bank
- ☎ 202/426–6821
- 🕐 Daily 8AM–midnight
- 🚇 Smithsonian, then 20-minute walk
- ♿ Excellent
- 💲 Free
- ↔ F. D. Roosevelt Memorial (► 57)

The Tidal Basin

The Jefferson Memorial was dedicated by President Franklin Delano Roosevelt on the 200th anniversary of Jefferson's birth, April 13, 1943. One of the best views of the White House can be had from the memorial's top steps.

Classical The Jefferson Memorial forms a north–south axis with the White House and, like virtually all building projects in Washington, it caused controversy in the capital city. Architect John Russell Pope adapted Rome's Pantheon in deference to Jefferson's love for classical architecture. Jefferson, an amateur architect himself, had used similar circular domed structures at his home, Monticello, and at the University of Virginia. But important Washingtonians derided Pope's design as old-fashioned, and some others argued that Jefferson's philosophy dictated a more utilitarian structure, perhaps an amphitheater. Eventually, the Pope memorial was dedicated in 1943 on Jefferson's 200th birthday.

Sculpture In front, a wide plaza overlooks the Tidal Basin with its cherry trees, famous for their spring blossom, and formal stairs lead up through a pedimented portico, surrounded by an Ionic colonnade encircling an open center. The pediment supports sculpted marble figures of Jefferson, Benjamin Franklin, John Adams, Roger Sherman, and Robert Livingston, members of the committee that drafted the Declaration of Independence. Rudolph Evans produced the 19-foot bronze sculpture of Jefferson in the center, and excerpts of his speeches and writings are carved into the walls.

U.S. HOLOCAUST MEMORIAL MUSEUM

This compelling memorial to the 11 million people killed by the Nazis between 1933 and 1945 graphically portrays both the personal stories and the wider issues of persecution and human tragedy. The museum sets new standards for design and historical interpretation.

Disturbing "You cannot deal with the Holocaust as a reasonable thing," explained architect James Ingo Freed. To that end, he created a discordant building, intended to disturb the classical and sometimes placid facades elsewhere in Washington. There are stunning high-tech audiovisuals, and computer technology documents and links survivors worldwide.

Nightmare Watchtowers line the north and south walls, contributing to the prison-like atmosphere, which prevails in the central atrium, the Hall of Witness, via exposed beams, metal railings, and malevolent elevators. A memory or a nightmare lurks everywhere you look or stand. The story that is told here is not of war but of humanity gone berserk. In so far as is possible, victims and survivors relate their experiences directly. You will find yourself horrified and shocked but compelled to continue, and grateful when provided with a place to rest and reflect. The Hall of Remembrance on the second floor provides just such a space, its filtered light and soaring stonework providing spiritual solace. A special exhibit for children under 12, *Daniel's Story*, re-creates what life was like for a young boy trapped in the downward spiral of Nazi occupation. The implicit question posed by the museum—the challenge of the visit—is not "Why did it happen?" but "How do we prevent similar occurrences?"

HIGHLIGHTS

- Unforgettable exhibition
- Hall of Remembrance
- Hall of Witness
- For children (8–12): *Daniel's Story*

INFORMATION

- ✛ G5
- ✉ 14th Street and Wallenberg Place SW, south of Independence Avenue
- 🕓 Daily 10–5:30. Closed Yom Kippur
- 🍴 Kosher restaurant
- Ⓠ Smithsonian
- ♿ Excellent
- 💷 Free
- ↔ Presidents' Memorials (► 26, 31, 32), Bureau of Engraving and Printing (► 35), Smithsonian Institution (► 36)
- ❓ Timed tickets distributed daily at 10AM; advance tickets through Protix ☎ 800/400–9373; line up early (before 9AM) or book two weeks in advance.

33

11

NATIONAL MUSEUM OF AMERICAN HISTORY

HIGHLIGHTS

- The "Star Spangled Banner"
- Hands-on-History Room
- Hands-on-Science Room
- *John Bull*
- Ruby slippers from the *Wizard of Oz*

INFORMATION

- ⊞ G5
- ✉ Constitution Avenue and 14th Street NW
- ☎ 202/357–2700
- ⊙ Daily 10–5:30
- 🍴 Cafeteria
- ⊕ Smithsonian, Federal Triangle
- ♿ Excellent
- ✋ Free
- ⟷ U.S. Holocaust Memorial Museum (▶ 33), Bureau of Engraving and Printing (▶ 35), Smithsonian Institution (▶ 36)
- ❓ Guided tours available

From the manuscript for the "Star Spangled Banner" and Judy Garland's ruby slippers to Duke Ellington's papers and inaugural ballgowns of the First Ladies—here are the objects that tell the story of America.

All-American Displays depict events and themes that define American life, such as "Field to Factory," recounting how African-Americans migrated from the agricultural South to industrial cities of the North. "A More Perfect Union" contributes to the dialogue about the U.S. Constitution, depicting the withdrawing of civil liberties from Japanese-Americans during World War II. The largest exhibition, "The Information Age," showcases automated gear ranging from early telephones to robotics to high-definition television. "From Parlor to Politics" and "First Ladies: Political Role and Public Image" depict women's political impact. An exhibition on time marks the millennium, while expansive displays on the Industrial Revolution and "Science in American Life" round out the offerings. Mail postcards from an original West Virginia general store; get your picture taken in front of the 280-ton steam engine *John Bull*, the country's oldest working locomotive; and, as an all-American finale, have an old-fashioned root beer float in the museum's ice cream parlor.

George Washington as a Greek god

BUREAU OF ENGRAVING & PRINTING

Usually when you visit a new city you don't make a beeline for a nondescript government building. This one is very different: children and adults alike delight in watching the powerful printing presses turn out more than $20 million every day.

Dollar bills It was in 1914 that the Bureau moved to this site from the redbrick Auditor's Building on a nearby corner. Today, all U.S. currency, stamps, presidential invitations, and military certificates are printed on the site: federal presses produce a staggering $100 billion annually, nearly all of which replaces currency already in circulation, in addition to 30 billion postage stamps. Any even slightly imperfect bills are summarily shredded. Also here is the grandly titled Office of Mutilated Currency, where citizens go to redeem bills partially destroyed by fire, flood, or laundry.

Printing presses After a film on the history of currency, you file past processing rooms where the bills are produced. The printing room turns out giant sheets of currency, made not from paper but from a cotton/linen fabric, each holding 32 bills, at a rate of 8,000 sheets an hour. The sheets are checked for any imperfections, trimmed, then stacked into bundles or 'bricks' of 4,000 notes ready for distribution to Federal Reserve Banks across the nation. The 35-minute self-guided tour ends at an exhibition hall filled with informative displays on the history of currency, counterfeiting, and stamps. Do not be daunted by the lines: they move rapidly. Outside, you'll find yourself near the Tidal Basin, one of the most beautiful spots in the city. Here you can rent a paddle boat and take a leisurely stroll along pathways lined with cherry trees—gorgeously pink in early spring.

HIGHLIGHTS

- Presses printing dollars
- Stacks of money, bundled for shipping
- Film on the history of currency
- Exhibition on stamps
- View of the Tidal Basin

INFORMATION

- ✛ G6
- ✉ 14 and C Streets SW
- ☎ 202/874–3019
- 🕐 Sep–May: Mon–Fri 9–2. Jun–Aug: Mon–Fri 9–2, 5–6:40
- Ⓢ Smithsonian
- ♿ Excellent
- 🎟 Free
- ↔ U.S. Holocaust Memorial Museum (➤ 33)
- ❓ Self-guided tours. Tickets required Apr–Sep, available 8AM–1:45PM at Wallenberg Place

13

FREER & ARTHUR M. SACKLER GALLERIES

FHIGHLIGHTS

The Freer Gallery of Art
- *Peacock Room*, James McNeill Whistler
- *Princess from the Land of Porcelain*, James McNeill Whistler
- Ancient Chinese artefacts
- Korean ceramics
- Japanese painted screens

The Arthur M. Sackler Gallery
- Chinese jades and bronzes
- Islamic manuscripts
- Ancient Iranian metalworks

INFORMATION

- ✚ G5
- ✉ 12th Street and Jefferson Drive or Independence Avenue, SW
- ☎ 202/357–2700
- ⏰ Daily 10–5
- Ⓜ Smithsonian
- ♿ Excellent
- 🎟 Free
- ↔ National Air and Space Museum (► 41), Hirshhorn Sculpture Garden (► 57)
- ❓ Guided tours Thu–Tue 11:30AM

Top: inside the Peacock Room, Freer Gallery

Right: James McNeill Whistler

One of the little-known treasures in the city, the Freer contains over 26,000 works of Asian art as well as one of the world's largest collections of paintings by James McNeill Whistler. The Sackler's collection of Asian art is complemented by exhibitions from all over the world.

Freer Gallery of Art Charles A. Platt designed this gray-granite palazzo-style building in 1923, which was renovated between 1988 and 1993. You can see Asian porcelains, Japanese screens, Chinese painting and bronzes, Korean stoneware, and Islamic art. James McNeill Whistler's blue and gold *Peacock Room* was inspired by the bird's striking plumage. It was decorated in 1876 for a London town house, and purchased by Freer, a friend of Whistler, in 1904.

Arthur M. Sackler Galler You can reach the Sackler Gallery by walking through an underground passage from the Freer or from Independence Avenue via a 1987 granite pavilion by Shepley Bullfinch Richardson and Abbott. Yes, the museum is underground (as is the National Museum of African Art across the plaza) but don't let that keep you away: a series of bridges and light wells alleviate any tomb-like aura and allow you to see the Islamic, Iranian, and Chinese, material from unexpected and unusual viewpoints.

SMITHSONIAN INSTITUTION

Tourists streaming off Metro escalators on summer mornings often ask commuters, "Where's the Smithsonian?" There is usually a suspicious silence on the visitor's part when the local answers: "Everything you see is the Smithsonian."

Benefactor An Englishman, James Smithson, stipulated that his estate should go "to the United States of America, to found at Washington, under the name of the Smithsonian Institution, an Establishment for the increase and diffusion of knowledge." After typical political wrangling, John Quincy Adams convinced Congress to take the gift, which was worth about $515,000 when it was accepted in 1846. Today the Smithsonian Institution comprises the largest cluster of museums in the world, as well as the National Zoo, and holds 140 million objects and specimens, with countless research projects worldwide on topics ranging from Russian voles and Native American baskets to endangered insects of the rain forests, aerodynamics, and molecular biology. The Smithsonian has 6,000 employees and an annual budget of nearly $400 million.

Castle Start your visit at James Renwick's iconic 1855 turreted, asymmetrical, red-sandstone castle—the Smithsonian's headquarters. The Crypt in the north foyer contains the body of James Smithson, moved here in 1904, while the large statue at the entrance is of the Smithsonian's first secretary, physicist Joseph Henry. The castle contains a state-of-the-art visitor information center, full of interactive maps, touch-screen programs, and brochures in several languages. Helpful volunteer guides help you plan your visit to the Smithsonian and other Washington sights.

HIGHLIGHTS

Mall Museums
- Arts and Industries Building
- Arther M. Sackler Gallery (➤ 36)
- Freer Gallery of Art (➤ 36)
- Hirshorn Museum and Sculpture garden (➤ 57)
- National Air and Space Museum (➤ 41)
- East and West wings of National Gallery of Art (➤ 40)
- National Museum of African Art
- National Museum of American History (➤ 34)
- National Museum of Natural History

Museums off the Mall
- Anacostia Museum
- National Postal Museum
- National Zoological Park (➤ 34)
- Renwick Gallery

INFORMATION

- ✠ G5–H5
- ✉ Jefferson Drive at 10th Street SW
- ☎ 202/357–2700
- ◷ Daily 10–5:30
- ⑪ The Commons for Smithsonian Members
- Ⓜ Smithsonian
- ♿ Excellent
- 👆 Free
- ❓ Film every 20 minutes

15

FBI BUILDING

HIGHLIGHTS

- Live-ammo demonstration
- FBI Most Wanted files
- FBI Most Famous Cases
- Exhibition of FBI History
- Fingerprint matching

INFORMATION

- G5
- E and 9th Streets NW
- 202/324–3447
- Mon–Fri 8:45–4:15
- Federal Triangle
- Excellent
- Free
- Smithsonian Institution (▶ 37), Ford's Theater (▶ 80)
- Tour every 20 minutes

FBI crest

Few subjects fascinate law-abiding Americans more than crime and crime prevention. It's not surprising, therefore, that for many visitors the FBI building is on the list of "ten most wanted" things to do in Washington.

Big Brother Stanley Gladych's modern, poured-concrete building—a 1974 example of the New Brutalism movement—conjures a Big Brother on Pennsylvania Avenue halfway between the Capitol and the White House. About 8,000 federal employees operate out of this looming structure, which fills an entire city block and embodies the "idea of a central core of files." Chartered in 1908, the FBI is the supreme federal authority on domestic crime. It deals with terrorism, organized crime, and industrial espionage, among other matters. Even today, the FBI's values are those of its most famous director, J. Edgar Hoover, who ran the agency from 1928 to 1972, an astounding 44 years. The FBI is the most respected investigative force in America, and its headquarters is one of the most popular tourist attractions in Washington: in other words be prepared for lines.

Wanted The tour takes in historical exhibits about famous cases the FBI has solved, an introduction to laboratory work including DNA analysis of hair fibers and blood samples, fingerprint matching, and a live-ammunition firearms demonstration followed by a question and answer session. Be alert when you visit: two of the FBI's most-wanted characters were fingered by tourists who saw the "Wanted" posters on the tour.

16

NATIONAL ARCHIVES

Walk through the building's colossal bronze entrance doors, up the sweeping staircase, and witness America through government archives: the Charters of Freedom, Civil War photographs, the gun that shot JFK, the Watergate tapes—it's all here.

Millions of documents John Russell Pope's *beaux-arts* building has served as the repository for all the nation's valuable official records since 1935. At last count it contained 3.2 billion textual documents, 1.6 million maps, 14.9 million photographs, and enough film and videotapes to encircle the globe many times.

Charters of Freedom After passing through a metal detector, you are led toward a throne-like structure in a domed rotunda with Corinthian columns and an arched pediment. Raised and enshrined at the center of the structure are the Declaration of Independence, the Constitution, and the Bill of Rights, sealed in bronze helium-filled cases covered with green ultraviolet filters. Forget about actually reading these Charters of Freedom, as they are called—the conservation techniques employed render it impossible, not to mention the steady stream of visitors patiently waiting their turn to cast their gaze upon the documents. At the end of each day, after all the visitors and researchers have gone home, the security staff lower the throne and the Charters into a bomb-proof vault beneath the exhibition floor. Also on exhibition are murals by Barry Faulkner entitled *The Declaration of Independence* and *The Constitution*. Changing exhibitions highlight the material — letters, photographs, and posters—from the vast collections maintained by the Archives.

HIGHLIGHTS

- Charters of Freedom
- Murals by Barry Faulkner
- Changing exhibition gallery

INFORMATION

- ✚ H5
- ✉ Constitution Avenue at 7th Street NW
- ☎ 202/501–5205
- 🕐 Daily 10–5:30
- Ⓜ Archives
- ♿ Excellent
- 💵 Free
- ↔ Smithsonian Institution (➤ 37), U.S. Botanic Gardens (➤ 42), U.S. Capitol (➤ 43)
- ❓ Tours daily at 10:15 and 1:15 (reservations required)

17

NATIONAL GALLERY OF ART

HIGHLIGHTS

- East Wing
- *Venus and Adonis*, Titian
- *The Alba Madonna*, Raphael
- *Laocoön*, El Greco
- *Daniel in the Lion's Den*, Rubens
- *Woman Holding a Balance*, Vermeer
- *A Girl with a Watering Can*, Renoir
- *Woman with a Parasol—Madame Monet and her Son*, Monet
- *The Skater*, Gilbert Stuart

INFORMATION

- H5
- Madison Drive between 3rd and 7th Streets NW
- 202/737–4215
- Mon–Sat 10–5; Sun 11–6
- Concourse Buffet, Cascade Café, Garden Café
- Archives
- Excellent
- Free
- National Air and Space Museum (➤ 41), U.S. Botanic Gardens (➤ 42), U.S. Capitol (➤ 43),
- Tours daily

Here you may see the U.S.'s only Leonardo da Vinci painting, **Ginevra,** *along with the world's top traveling exhibitions. When you think that every American citizen owns an equal share of the art here, you may well feel a burst of patriotic pride.*

Vision   When Andrew Mellon was secretary of the treasury (1921–32), he realized that the capital city lacked a great gallery highlighting the development of Western art. So when he died in 1937 he left an endowment and his renowned collection of paintings and sculpture to the American people, and passed on his dream to his son. Paul Mellon oversaw the construction of John Russell Pope's Classical-Revival building, opened in 1941 and eventually of I.M. Pei's stunning East Wing, opened in 1978, and perhaps the most beautiful modern building in America.

Western art   The permanent collection includes Renaissance painting, with works by Italian grand masters Raphael and Titian, Spanish painters Velasquez, El Greco, and Goya as well as Flemish, German, and Dutch paintings from van der Weyden and Dürer to Rubens and Vermeer. The French are abundantly represented by Watteau, Corot, Manet, Renoir, and all the Pre-, Neo- and Post-Impressionists. Works by William Hogarth begin the tour of British painting, from Gainsborough to Turner. American painting is represented by Gilbert Stuart, Winslow Homer, James McNeill Whistler, and others. Also on offer are films and lectures on the works of art, while you can access information about the museum's paintings in the Micro Gallery's user-friendly computerized collection. Outside, a sculpture garden, opened in 1999, includes works by Roy Lichtenstein and Claes Oldenburg, and a huge bronze spider by Louise Bourgeois.

NATIONAL AIR & SPACE MUSEUM

The most visited museum in the world takes parents and children alike on a pioneering journey from the first manned motorized flight to the most recent space exploration—"infinity and beyond!"

Flight pioneers This museum was the Smithsonian's bicentennial gift to the nation. More than ten million visitors a year explore its monumental glass and granite galleries. The collection—begun as early as 1861, when the first secretary of the Smithsonian urged experiments in balloon flight—today includes the Wright Brothers' 1903 *Flyer;* Charles Lindbergh's *Spirit of St. Louis;* Chuck Yeager's *Bell X-1*, in which he broke the sound barrier; and *The Voyager*, in which Dick Rutan and Jeana Yeager flew nonstop around the world.

Into space Among the spectacular rockets, missiles, and space vehicles on view in the Space Halls you'll see the Columbia Space Shuttle, the Apollo-Soyuz spacecraft, Skylab, and lunar exploration vehicles. Also here is the *Enola Gay*, the plane that carried the atomic bomb dropped on Hiroshima, Japan at the end of World War II.

HIGHLIGHTS

- Wright Brothers' 1903 *Flyer*
- Charles Lindbergh's *Spirit of St. Louis*
- Chuck Yeager's *Bell X-1 Glamorous Glennis*
- Soviet *Sputnik*
- John Glenn's *Friendship* and *Apollo 11*
- Columbia Space Shuttle
- Skylab
- Lunar Exploration Vehicles

INFORMATION

- H5
- Independence Avenue at 6th Street SW
- 202/357–2700
- Daily 10–5:30
- Wright Place Cafeteria
- L'Enfant Plaza
- Excellent
- Free. Einstein Planetarium: Moderate
- National Gallery of Art (➤ 40), U.S. Botanic Gardens (➤ 42)
- Langley Theatre, IMAX: films every 35 minutes

Spirit of St. Louis, *flown by Charles Lindbergh*

19

U.S. BOTANIC GARDENS

HIGHLIGHTS

- Seasonal displays
- Orchids and tropical plants
- Coffee, chocolate, and banyan trees
- Bartholdi Fountain

INFORMATION

- ✚ H5
- ✉ 1st Street SW and Maryland Avenue
- ☎ 202/225–7099
- ⏰ Daily 9–5. Under renovation at press time; call before you visit
- 🚇 Federal Center SW
- ♿ Excellent
- 💵 Free
- ↔ Smithsonian Institution (► 36), U.S. Capitol (► 43)

December's poinsettia display is an annual must for many Washingtonians. If you visit on a weekday morning in winter, when you may well be alone in the desert display, you can easily imagine yourself in Arizona or the Sahara.

Exotic glasshouse U.S. explorers in the 19th century needed a place to conserve the specimens they brought home from the South Seas, so Congress authorized the first greenhouse in 1842. The present 40,000-square-foot conservatory, an attractive combination of iron-and-glass greenhouse and stone orangeries, at the southwestern corner of Capitol Hill, was erected in 1931.

Flowers for all seasons The entrance hall serves as a seasonal gallery displaying by turns Christmas poinsettias, tulips and hyacinths, or chrysanthemums. Not far away there is a permanent planting of high desert flora as well as a steamy tropical exhibit in the large glass pavilion. In two smaller conservatories on either side you can see orchids, as well as coffee, chocolate and banyan trees, and plants resembling those on earth during the Jurassic period 200 million years ago. If you can ignore traffic whizzing by, you'll appreciate the tiny pocket park across Independence Avenue, operated by the Botanic Gardens. It is arguably the most beautiful in the city. Here, plantings frame and showcase the cast-iron Bartholdi Fountain (1876), embellished with sea nymphs, monsters, tritons, and lighted globes; it was designed by Frédéric-Auguste Bartholdi, best known as the sculptor of the Statue of Liberty, for the Philadelphia Centennial Exhibition, intending it to represent the elements of light and water. The tables on the Summer Terrace are used for picnics.

U.S. CAPITOL

Imitated on state buildings throughout the country, the dome of the U.S. Capitol makes an iconic backdrop for television newscasters and politicians who want to associate their pronouncements with a stirring symbol of American democracy.

Icon The dome was an engineering feat when undertaken in 1851 by Capitol architect Charles Walter and U.S. Army Quartermaster General Montgomery Meigs. It became a political symbol before it was half finished: the Civil War broke out while it was under construction, and the Capitol housed the wounded and their caregivers. Many advised President Lincoln to halt work on the building, but he was adamant that progress continue as "a sign we intend the Union shall go on." The 9-million-pound cast-iron dome, rising 280 feet, was completed in 1863.

Founding fathers You may wait in the Great Rotunda for a guided tour, or wander freely in the public spaces. The paintings overhead were done from life and from memory by George Washington's aide, John Trumbull. *The Apotheosis of Washington*, a fresco by Constantino Brumidi, depicts classical deities and the Founding Fathers. Brumidi, it was said, consorted with "ladies of the night," whose likenesses then appeared as ample maidens ministering to George Washington. When Congress is in session, you may visit the House or Senate chambers.

HIGHLIGHTS

● Rotunda
● Frescoes by Constantino Brumidi
● Paintings by John Trumbull
● Visit to the House or Senate Chambers

INFORMATION

✚ J5
✉ 1st Street between Independence and Constitution Avenues
☎ 202/225–6827
🕐 Daily 9–4:30
🍴 Capitol Cafeteria, Dining Room
Ⓜ Capitol South
♿ Excellent
🎫 Free
↔ U.S. Botanic Gardens (➤ 42), Union Station (➤ 44), U.S. Supreme Court Building (➤ 45), Library of Congress (➤ 46)
❓ Tours daily, every 15 minutes. A pass to observe a session of Congress can be obtained from a senator's or representative's office by U.S. nationals. Foreign visitors apply at the ground-floor appointment desk. When Congress works overtime, the exterior dome light in the cupola is lit. Visitors are welcome on a first come, first served basis

The dome's colonnade   43

21

UNION STATION

HIGHLIGHTS

- Main Hall
- Statues of Roman legionnaires
- East Hall
- Presidential Waiting Room
- Columbus Plaza

INFORMATION

- J4
- 50 Massachusetts Avenue NE
- 202/371–9441
- 24 hours for train service; stores, restaurants, and theaters vary
- Many
- Union Station
- Excellent
- Free
- U.S. Capitol and Capitol Hill attractions (▶ 43)

The beautiful Union Station, now housing shops, restaurants and a cinema as well as the railway, is a treasure for all: movie-going teenagers, office workers doing errands at lunch, dining dealmakers, commuting bureaucrats, and tourists taking in the sights.

World's largest Architect Daniel H. Burnham lived up to his motto, "Make No Little Plans", when he undertook the consolidation of the District's several train lines early last century. Burnham's vaulted, white-marble, *beaux-arts* Union Station was the largest train station in the world when it opened in 1907. Renovated and reopened in 1988, it is now filled with a huge variety of restaurants and sophisticated boutiques. There are nine movie screens, and it is both an active train terminal and a Metro stop.

More than trains Inside, thousands of travelers pass under a cavernous 96-foot-high coffered ceiling, embellished with gold leaf and guarded by 46 Augustus Saint-Gaudens statues of Roman legionnaires. The original Presidential Waiting Room is now a restaurant. The market-like East Hall has stalls selling items from around the world. Outside, a grand memorial to Christopher Columbus by Lorado Taft fronts the massive Doric colonnade, and allegorical neoclassical sculptures depicting fire, electricity, and mechanics set off the skyline. You can visit another restored Burnham building to the right: the Old Post Office, which now houses the Smithsonian Postal Museum. To the left, you can see an example of contemporary *beaux-arts* styling in the architect Edward Larrabee Barnes's new Thurgood Marshall Federal Judicial Center.

U.S. SUPREME COURT BUILDING

One of the justices called this 1935 neo-classical building, designed by Cass Gilbert, Jr., in gleaming Vermont marble, "bombastically pretentious...for a quiet group of old boys such as the Supreme Court."

Judgments   Since the arrival of Justices Sandra Day O'Conner and Ruth Bader Ginsburg, the Court is no longer an old boys' ghetto, and it has never really been quiet. The 1857 Dred Scott decision, which held that Congress had no authority to limit slavery, contributed to the onset of the Civil War. Rulings on abortion have frequently made the plaza in front of the building, one of Washington's most impressive Greek temples, a focus of civil disobedience. *Brown v. Board of Education* required the integration of schools and bus travel across the land, and *Engel v. Vitale* outlawed school prayer. But in another way, the Court does work quietly. Justices are appointed for life and rarely give interviews. The Court is not televised, and information never leaks out of the building, as is common elsewhere in the city.

Law in action   The steps up to the colonnaded entrance are flanked by two white marble allegorical figures by James Earle Fraser depicting *The Contemplation of Justice* and *The Authority of Law*. The magnificent bronze entrance doors, designed by John Donnely, Jr., and weighing 13 tons, lead into the huge entrance hall with busts of all the former chief justices. When the Court is in session, you can join the "three-minute line" and glimpse proceedings from the Standing Gallery. A statue of John Marshall, Chief Justice from 1755–1835, dominates the ground floor where a short film and changing exhibits describe the work of the Court.

HIGHLIGHTS

- Bronze entrance doors
- Plaza sculpture
- Busts of chief justices
- Film and exhibits on Court history
- Statue of Justice John Marshall
- The Court in session

INFORMATION

- ✚ J5
- ✉ 1st and East Capitol Streets NE
- ☎ 202/479–3211
- 🕐 Mon–Fri 9–4:30
- 🍴 Cafeteria
- Ⓔ Capitol South, Union Station
- ♿ Excellent
- 🎫 Free
- ↔ U.S. Capitol (➤ 43), Library of Congress (➤ 46)
- ❓ Lectures on the half-hour when the Court is not in session

Spring blossom softens the stern facade

23

LIBRARY OF CONGRESS

HIGHLIGHTS

- *Torch of Learning* on green copper dome
- *Beaux-arts* design
- Main Reading Room
- Sculpture inside and out
- View of the Capitol from the Madison Building cafeteria

INFORMATION

- ➕ J5
- ✉ 1st Street and Independence Avenue SE
- ☎ 202/707–5458
- 🕐 Mon–Sat 10–5
- 🍴 Cafeteria, coffee shop, Montpelier Restaurant
- 🚇 Capitol South
- ♿ Excellent. Visitor Services ☎ 202/707–9779 provides American Sign Language interpretation
- 🎫 Free
- ↔ U.S. Capitol (➤ 43), U.S. Supreme Court Building (➤ 45)
- ❓ Tours begin at the Jefferson Building Mon–Sat 11, 1, 2:30, 4. Library resources are open to anyone over 18 pursuing research. Regular changing exhibitions

Libraries and bookstores are one of Washington's big draws. The Library of Congress is the mother lode—it's the world's largest library and the U.S.'s national library—with over 115 million items on 600 miles of shelves.

Room to read Congress appropriated funds for a library in 1800. Unfortunately, it was destroyed by the British when they sacked the Capitol in 1814. Thomas Jefferson's personal library then became the nucleus of the new collection. The 1897 imposing granite *beaux-arts* Jefferson Building has a ceremonial portico, Corinthian columns, and sculpted busts of men of letters gazing down. For many scholars, sitting in the Main Reading Room at the mahogany readers' tables 160 feet below the domed ceiling is an almost spiritual experience. The Art Deco Adams building was completed in 1939; the modern Madison building opposite in 1980.

Not just books Holdings in the Jefferson, Madison, and Adams buildings, clustered between 1st and 3rd Streets on Pennsylvania Avenue SE, include the contents of Lincoln's pockets on the evening he was shot, original scores by Beethoven and Brahms, props belonging to Houdini, a Gutenberg Bible, and original drafts of the Declaration of Independence, the Emancipation Proclamation and the Gettysburg Address. If you've got a special interest, a librarian will arrange for you to see relevant artefacts.

The copper dome and Torch of Learning

24

SHRINE OF THE IMMACULATE CONCEPTION

The largest Catholic church in the U.S., and the eighth largest in the world, is big, ordered and crisp. Renowned for its beautiful mosaics, it is dedicated to Christ's mother, Mary, named Patroness of the United States by Pope Pius IX in 1847.

Construction Work began on the grounds of Catholic University in 1920. The ground-level Crypt Church was completed in 1926. After the Great Depression and World War II, construction began again in earnest during 1954, and the Great Upper Church was dedicated on November 20, 1959.

American saint Separating the Crypt Church from the Chapel of Our Lady of Hostyn is a supremely delicate stained-glass screen depicting scenes from the life of Saint John Neumann, the first American man to have been admitted to the sainthood. The Byzantine-style dome, 237 feet in height and 108 feet in diameter, is lavishly decorated with symbols of the Virgin Mary picked out in gold leaf and colored majolica tiles. The 329-foot-high bell tower houses a 56-bell carillon cast in France and supports a 20-foot gilded cross visible in every direction for miles around.

Interior Three rose windows embellished with gold and amethyst illuminate the sanctuary, along with ranks of other windows depicting the lives of Mary, the Holy Family, the saints, and redeemed sinners. Sculpture includes George Carr's 37-ton marble *Universal Call to Holiness* on the south wall of the Great Upper Church. But the lasting image is of the extraordinary mosaics—acres of them on ceilings and walls, in the apse and in the chapels—donated by American Catholics.

HIGHLIGHTS

- Ecclesiastical sculpture
- Mosaics

INFORMATION

✚ Off map, north of K1
✉ 4th Street and Michigan Avenue NE
☎ 202/526–8300
🕐 Apr–Oct: daily 7–7. Nov–Mar: daily 7–6
🍴 Cafeteria daily 7:30–2
Ⓜ Brookland
♿ Excellent
💲 Free
❓ Tours by appointment, Mon–Sat 9–noon, 1–3; Sun 1:30–3

The Byzantine-style Christ in the dome

47

CEDAR HILL

HIGHLIGHTS

- Harriet Beecher Stowe's desk
- Rocking chair, gift of Republic of Haiti
- Portraits of Elizabeth Cady Stanton and Susan B. Anthony
- View of Washington

INFORMATION

- ➕ L8
- ✉ 1411 W Street SE
- ☎ 202/426–5961
- 🕐 Mid-Apr–mid-Oct: daily 9–5. Mid-Oct–mid-Apr: 9–4
- 🚌 By Tourmobile (mid-Jun–Labor Day and Feb: daily) ☎ 202/554–7950
  By car 11th Street Bridge to Martin Luther King Avenue, left on W Street
- ♿ Good
- 💵 Inexpensive
- ❓ Hourly guided tours: daily 9–4. Reservation ☎ 800/365–2267

Statue of Frederick Douglass

Built in 1854, the attractive Italianate country house known as Cedar Hill was the last home of abolitionist Frederick Douglass. Decorative arts, libraries and family mementos provide an intimate look at his life and work.

Slave America's famous abolitionist was born into slavery in Maryland in about 1818, and was separated from his mother at birth. Years later he wrote that he had never seen her in daylight during the seven years before she died as she had had to walk to see him and return between the end of one work day and sun up the next. Douglass, badly treated by a plantation overseer, was apprenticed by his owner as a ship caulker but he ran away, becoming active in the Massachusetts antislavery movement, and publishing his first autobiography in 1845. He fled to Europe to avoid slave bounty hunters, where British friends bought him his freedom. He lectured and published widely on antislavery topics, became an adviser to President Lincoln, an ambassador to Haiti, and a staunch supporter of women's suffrage. When he moved into Cedar Hill, he was the first black resident of Anacostia, breaking the prohibition against "Irish, Negro, mulatto, or persons of African blood", according to a developer's advert of the day.

Viewpoint Cedar Hill, now the Frederick Douglass National Historic Site, occupies the highest point in Anacostia, with a great view of the Anacostia River and the capital. Among the many artifacts on display inside the house is the desk at which Harriet Beecher Stowe wrote *Uncle Tom's Cabin*. The National Park Service, that manages the house, maintains an information center and a bookstore specializing in African-American titles.

WASHINGTON's
best

AFRICAN-AMERICAN SITES

1212 T Street NW, the house where "Duke" Ellington grew up in the early 1900s

Black Broadway

Since the area was torched in the 1968 riots sparked by Martin Luther King, Jr.'s assassination, U Street NW has been transformed. The reopening in 1994 of the 1,250-seat Lincoln Theater caps the renaissance and the strip once again deserves the appellation "Black Broadway." *Community Rhythms*, the vibrant murals of artist Al Smith, decorate the U Street–Cardozo Metro entrances and depict the area's regeneration.

See Top 25 Sights for
CEDAR HILL (➤ 48)
LINCOLN MEMORIAL (➤ 26)

AFRICAN-AMERICAN CIVIL WAR MEMORIAL AND MUSEUM

In a historic Masonic Temple, this museum tells the story of the 209,145 African-Americans who fought to abolish slavery in the American Civil War. Edward Hamilton's bronze memorial was dedicated in 1999.

✚ G2 ✉ 1000 U Street NW ☎ 202/667–2667 ⏰ Museum daily 9–5. Memorial 24 hours 🚇 U Street–Cardozo 🎟 Free

ANACOSTIA MUSEUM

Although closed for renovations through 2001, you can see its African-American exhibits at the Smithsonian's Arts and Industries Building.

✚ G5 ✉ 900 Jefferson Drive ☎ 202/357–2700 ⏰ Daily 10–5 🚇 Smithsonian 🎟 Free

EDWARD KENNEDY "DUKE" ELLINGTON RESIDENCE

Though born at 1217 22nd Street NW, "Duke" Ellington (1899–1974, ➤ 12) grew up on this street and took piano lessons nearby.

✚ G2 ✉ 1212 T Street NW ⏰ Not open to the public 🚇 U Street–Cardozo

FATHER PATRICK FRANCIS HEALY BUILDING, GEORGETOWN UNIVERSITY

This 1879 baronial fantasy honors the first black Catholic priest and bishop in America, who later became president of Georgetown University.

✚ C3 ✉ 37th and O Streets NW ☎ 202/687–5055 ⏰ 24 hours 🚇 Rosslyn, then bus No. 38B 🎟 Free

FREDERICK DOUGLASS HOUSE

The first Washington home of one of the country's most celebrated abolitionists, now part of the Smithsonian.

✚ K5 ✉ 316 A Street NE ⏰ Not open to the public 🚇 Capitol South

HOWARD UNIVERSITY

Chartered in 1867 to educate freed men and women, Howard is the alma mater of Thurgood Marshall, associate justice of the Supreme Court. It occupies 89 acres and houses 12,000 students pursuing nearly 200 areas of study. The law school is widely acknowledged as the place where African-Americans learned how to use the legal system to drive the civil rights movement in the 1960s.

✚ H2 ✉ 2400 6th Street NW ☎ 202/806–6100 ⏰ Mon–Fri 9–5 🚇 Shaw–Howard University

INDUSTRIAL BANK OF WASHINGTON

At the beginning of the 20th century, white banks accepted deposits from black people but would not make loans to them, so when John L. Lewis opened his bank in 1913, it soon became known as "the wage earners' bank." In 1932 Texan Jesse Mitchell opened Industrial on this site with $200,000; the bank still serves Washington's African-American community.
✚ G2 ✉ 2000 11th Street NW ☎ 202/722–2050 🕓 Mon–Thu 9–3; Fri 9–3, 4:30–6; Sat 9–noon 🚇 U Street–Cardozo

LINCOLN PARK

Charlotte Scott, a Virginia woman, contributed the first $5 toward the Emancipation Memorial, which was supported entirely from funds from free blacks. Dedicated on April 14, 1876, it remained the city's only monument to Abraham Lincoln until 1922, when the Lincoln Memorial was dedicated. In 1974, the Emancipation Memorial was turned away from the Capitol, to face the new Mary McLeod Bethune Memorial (► 12).
✚ K5 ✉ East Capitol Street between 11th and 13th Streets 🚇 Eastern Market

TRUE REFORMERS HALL

Architect John A. Lankford's six-story 1903 building housed a variety of black-owned retail stores, offices, entertainments, and a drill room and armory for Washington's black National Guard unit. It later housed a popular dance hall, where Duke Ellington (► 12 and 50) performed with his band, Duke's Serenaders.
✚ G2 ✉ 1200 U Street NW 🕓 Not open to the public 🚇 U Street–Cardozo

National Council of Negro Women

The Mary McLeod Bethune Museum and Archives (► 54) house the records of the National Council of Negro Women, founded in 1935, and uniting the considerable influence of hundreds of African-American women's groups. These women shaped public policy regarding civil rights, health care, housing, and employment, extending even to the formation of the United Nations.

Mary McLeod Bethune Memorial, Lincoln Park

MARY McLEOD BETHUNE
1875 1955
Let her works praise her

FOR CHILDREN

See Top 25 Sights for
BUREAU OF ENGRAVING AND PRINTING (➤ 35)
FBI BUILDING (➤ 38)
NATIONAL GEOGRAPHIC SOCIETY, EXPLORERS HALL (➤ 29)
UNION STATION (➤ 44)

Information Sources

The Washington Post "Carousel Weekend" lists local events for children. WKDL radio (1050 AM) caters to children and their parents and often reports on children's events.

THE SMITHSONIAN MUSEUMS

These museums entertain and educate millions of children every year on everything from aardvarks and airplanes to singing insects and space suits. Of special interest are the dinosaurs and the insect zoo at the National Museum of Natural History; the Hands-on-History and Hands-on-Science rooms at the National Museum of American History (➤ 34); "Amazonia" and the Invertebrate House at the National Zoological Park (➤ 53); the IMAX films at the National Air and Space Museum (➤ 41); and the Discovery Theater with its puppet shows, plays, and storytelling.

National Museum of Natural History 🔢 G5 ✉ Constitution Avenue and 10th Street NW ☎ 202/357–2700 🕐 Daily 10–5.30 🚇 Smithsonian, Federal Triangle 💰 Free

National Museum of American History 🔢 G5 ✉ Constitution Avenue and 14th Street NW ☎ 202/357–2700 🕐 Daily 10–5.30 🚇 Smithsonian, Federal Triangle 💰 Free

National Zoological Park 🔢 E1–F1 ✉ 3001 Connecticut Avenue NW ☎ 202/673–4717 🕐 Daily 6–6 🚇 Woodley Park–Zoo 💰 Free

National Air and Space Museum 🔢 H5 ✉ Independence Avenue at 6th Street SW ☎ 202/357–2700 🕐 Daily 10–5:30 🚇 L'Enfant Plaza 💰 Free

Discovery Theater 🔢 G5 ✉ 900 Jefferson Drive SW ☎ 200/357–1500 🕐 Plays Mon–Fri: 10AM, 11:30AM 🚇 Smithsonian 💰 Inexpensive

The National Museum of American History

CAPITAL CHILDREN'S MUSEUM

Here, everything is as messy as if a horde of happy children had played with everything for years—and they have. Permanent exhibitions explore Mexican and Thai cultures, animation, still-life drawing and children's art, and children's health and well-being.
🔢 J4 ✉ 800 3rd Street NE ☎ 202/675–4120 🕐 Daily 10–5 🚌 6 🚇 Union Station 💰 Inexpensive

HARD ROCK CAFÉ

Kids and their parents love the up-beat rock and roll hall of fame atmosphere and good-sized portions at this restaurant, complete with its own line of T-shirts and baseball caps.
🔢 G4 ✉ 999 E Street NW ☎ 202/737–7625 🕐 Mon–Fri 11AM–midnight; Sat, Sun 11AM–1AM 🚇 Metro Center

NATIONAL AQUARIUM

Opened in 1873, the aquarium has a touch tank, sea

turtles, eels, tropical, and freshwater fish, and shark
and piranha feeding at 2 o'clock on alternate days.

🚩 G5 ✉ 14th Street and Pennsylvania Avenue NW ☎ 202/482–
2825 🕙 Daily 9–5 🚇 Federal Triangle 💶 Inexpensive

NATIONAL ZOOLOGICAL PARK

Within the 160 acres landscaped by Frederick Law
Olmsted, Sr., in 1889, zoo designers have constantly
renovated enclosures to provide natural settings for
birds, hoofed stock, komodo dragons, pygmy
hippopotamuses, big cats, monkeys, and much more.
The quiet Invertebrate House houses many rarely
seen animals.

🚩 E1–F1 ✉ 3001 Connecticut Avenue NW ☎ 202/673–4717
🕙 Grounds daily 6AM–6:15PM. Animal buildings May–mid-Sep: daily
10–6. Mid-Sep–Apr: daily 10–4:30. "Amazonia" daily 10–4 🍴 Snack
bars 🚇 Woodley Park–Zoo 💶 Free, but parking charge

NAVY MUSEUM

Big ships, cannons, submarines, and periscopes; kids
here can pretend to conquer the seven seas.

🚩 K7 ✉ 9th and M Streets SE, Building 76 ☎ 202/433–4882
🕙 Mon–Fri 9–4; Sat, Sun, hols 10–5 🚇 Eastern Market, Navy Yard
💶 Free

PLANET HOLLYWOOD

Owned by movie stars, including Sylvester Stallone
and Bruce Willis, and decorated with cinema memorabilia, this restaurant specializes in burgers,
pasta, and other American favorites. A merchandising
arm sells everything from caps to jackets.

🚩 G5 ✉ 1101 Pennsylvania Avenue NW ☎ 202/783–7827
🕙 Daily 11AM–10:30PM 🚇 Federal Triangle

PUPPET COMPANY PLAYHOUSE

Located in Glen Echo Park, MD, this troupe
presents plays beloved by children of all ages.

🚩 Off map at A1 ✉ 7300 MacArthur Boulevard, Glen Echo, MD
☎ 301/320–6668 💶 Inexpensive; free annual puppet exhibition
🚌 Ride on bus 29

SHOPPING FOR KIDS

FAO Schwarz stocks the best (or at least the most
expensive) toys, dolls, children's books, and more.

🚩 D3 ✉ 3222 M Street NW ☎ 202/342–2285 🕙 Mon–Sat
10–9; Sun 11–6 🍴 Café

WASHINGTON DOLLS' HOUSE AND TOY
MUSEUM

This museum has an extensive collection of Victorian
dolls, dollhouses, toys, and games.

🚩 Off map at D1 ✉ 5236 44th Street NW ☎ 202/244–0024
🕙 Tue–Sat 10–5; Sun noon–5 🚇 Friendship Heights
💶 Inexpensive

*Tigers and other
endangered species are
bred at Washington's
National Zoological Park*

Baby-sitters

For sitters, check with your hotel
concierge or call:

Mothers' Aides Inc.

✉ Box 7088, Fairfax Station, VA
22039 ☎ 703/250–0700

WeeSit

✉ 10681 Oak Thrust Court,
Burke, VA 22015

☎ 703/764–1542.

LIBRARIES & ARCHIVES

See Top 25 Sights for
LIBRARY OF CONGRESS (► 46)
NATIONAL ARCHIVES (► 39)

A bookworm's paradise

When listing the reasons to live inside the Capital Beltway, many Washingtonians praise the literary scene. Museums and historic sites have acres of bookshelves, crammed with publications related to museum collections and historic events, and most have libraries open to researchers. Throughout the city, specialized collections are open to anyone with an interest and some time, as well as scholars and students of everything from Jewish-American military history to Shakespeare.

BETHUNE MUSEUM AND ARCHIVES

Preserving and documenting African-American women's participation in American history is the mission of this site in a Victorian townhouse near historic Logan Circle. Mary McLeod Bethune, political activist, educator, and founder of the National Council of Negro Women, once lived here; the house also served as the Council's headquarters.

➕ G3 ✉ 1318 Vermont Avenue NW ☎ 202/332–1233 🕐 Sep–May: Mon–Fri 10–4. Jun–Aug: Mon–Sat 10–4 🚇 U Street–Cardozo, McPherson Square 🎫 Free

FOLGER SHAKESPEARE LIBRARY

The world's most comprehensive collection of Shakespeare's works is included in this collection of 275,000 books, manuscripts, and paintings from and about the European Renaissance.

➕ J5 ✉ 201 E Capitol SE ☎ 202/544–4600 🕐 For researchers Mon–Fri 10–4. Guided tours Mon–Fri 11 AM; Sat 11AM, 1PM 🎫 Free 🚇 Capitol South

HISTORICAL SOCIETY OF WASHINGTON

Text and image collections relating to D.C.'s social history are housed in the ornate Victorian Heurich Mansion, built by a wealthy brewer.

➕ F3 ✉ 1307 New Hampshire Avenue NW ☎ 202/785–2068 🕐 Mon–Sat 10–4 🚇 Dupont Circle 🎫 Inexpensive

MARTIN LUTHER KING MEMORIAL LIBRARY

The large, active main branch of the D.C. public library system, M.L.K. has an extensive Washingtoniana collection, as well as a Black Studies Division. Mies van der Rohe designed the unadorned steel-and-glass building, which opened in 1972 and is softened by Don Miller's mural celebrating the life of Martin Luther King, Jr.

➕ G4 ✉ 901 G Street NW ☎ 202/727–1111 🕐 Mon–Thu 10–9; Fri, Sat 10–5:30; Sun 1–5 🚇 Gallery Place

MOORLAND-SPINGARN RESEARCH CENTER

The Center includes extensive archives and secondary material about the African diaspora.

➕ H2 ✉ 500 Howard Place in Founders Library, Howard University ☎ 202/806–7239 🕐 Mon–Fri 9–4:45 🚇 Shaw–Howard University

NATIONAL GEOGRAPHIC SOCIETY LIBRARY

This little-known library houses 50,000 books on geography, natural history, travel, and topics that have long interested the Society, such as polar exploration.

Of course, all the Society's publications, including a complete run of the famous yellow magazine begun in 1888, are available. The reading room has an automated catalog, good light, and warm wood paneling.

➕ F3 ✉ 17th and M Streets NW ☎ 202/857–7783 ◷ By appointment, Mon–Fri 1:30–5 Ⓜ Dupont Circle, Farragut North

SMITHSONIAN INSTITUTION LIBRARIES
Collections include images of airplanes of all periods, worldwide biological flora and fauna, space, film and television, linguistics, paleobiology, the history of railroads, women's political life, domestic industry, war, peace, and everything in between. Of special note are the Archives of American Art, the National Anthropological Archives, and the Human Studies Film Archives (➤ 37). Contact the Smithsonian's headquarters at the Castle for opening times of individual libraries.

➕ G5 ✉ The Castle, Jefferson Drive at 10th Street SW ☎ 202/357–2700 ◷ Daily 9–5:30 Ⓜ Smithsonian

SUMNER SCHOOL MUSEUM AND ARCHIVES
Architect Adolph Cluss won a Medal for Progress at the Vienna World's Exposition in 1873 for his innovative use of hallways and closets to shield classrooms from exterior noise. The school stood as a model example of black education during segregation. It now houses the archives of the D.C. Public Schools.

➕ F3 ✉ 17th and M Streets NW ☎ 202/727–3419 ◷ Mon–Sat 10–5 Ⓜ Dupont Circle

Exhibits at the National Geographic Society

55

GARDENS, SCULPTURE & MEN ON HORSES

Do not let the Washington summer heat keep you from exploring the city's often inspiring, often whimsical sculptures, many of them in lovely gardens with plenty of shade.

Friendship Arch

Located at Chinatown Metro, this gilded arch symbolizes the energy and vitality of Washington's Asian community.

➕ H4 ✉ Chinatown, 7th and G Streets NW 🕐 24 hours 🚇 Gallery Place–Chinatown 🎟 Free

See Top 25 Sights for
BARTHOLDI FOUNTAIN AT THE U.S. BOTANIC GARDENS (► 42)
COLUMBUS PLAZA AT UNION STATION (► 44)
JEFFERSON MEMORIAL (► 32)
LINCOLN MEMORIAL (► 26)
NEPTUNE'S COURT AT THE LIBRARY OF CONGRESS (► 46)
VIETNAM VETERANS MEMORIAL AND CONSTITUTION GARDENS (► 28)
WASHINGTON MONUMENT (► 31)

THE AWAKENING

The Awakening, by J. Seward Johnson, was originally part of a temporary exhibition. So many Washingtonians appreciated the bearded aluminum giant rising from the tip of Hains Point that it stayed. The surrounding park has jogging and bike paths, tennis, swimming, and golf.

➕ H9 ✉ Hains Point, East Potomac Park ☎ 202/485–9880, 202/727–6523 🕐 24 hours 🚇 Waterfront 🎟 Free

BISHOPS GARDEN

Designed around European ruins and a statue of the Prodigal Son, this is a gem in the 57 acres at Washington National Cathedral. Plantings include herbs, boxwood, magnolia trees, and tea roses.

➕ C1–D1 ✉ Wisconsin and Massachusetts Avenues NW ☎ 202/537–6200 🕐 May–Labor Day: Mon–Fri 10–9; Sat, Sun 10–4:30. Labor Day–Apr: daily 10–4:30 🚇 Tenley Town; 30 series bus south 🎟 Free

DUMBARTON OAKS

In 1944, the international conference leading to the formation of the United Nations was held at this estate, also known for its fine 10-acre formal garden. The orangery, rose garden, wisteria, magnificent old shade and terraced vistas make this a must-see for anyone interested in gardens, or who wants to rest for just a few moments surrounded by blazing nature.

➕ D2 ✉ 31st and R Streets NW ☎ 202/339–6400 🕐 Daily 2–5 🚇 Dupont Circle, then bus No. D2 🎟 Inexpensive

EINSTEIN MEMORIAL

In the grounds of Washington's National Academy of Sciences, Robert Berks's sculpture depicts the physicist Albert Einstein gently feeding birds and inviting children onto his lap.

⊞ E5 ⊠ 22nd Street NW and Constitution Avenue, in the grounds of the National Academy of Sciences ⏰ 24 hours 🚇 Foggy Bottom 💵 Free

FDR MEMORIAL
Dedicated in 1997, the memorial to Franklin Delano Roosevelt consists of ten bronze sculptures set in 7½ acres around the Tidal Basin near the Lincoln, Vietnam, and Korean War Memorials. They depict Franklin Delano and Eleanor Roosevelt, and events from the Great Depression and World War II.
⊞ F6 ⊠ West Potomac Park ☎ 202/228–2491 ⏰ Daylight hours 🚇 Smithsonian, then 30-minute walk 💵 Free

GRANT MEMORIAL
General Ulysses S. Grant looks weary from his struggles as he sits on horseback at the foot of Capitol Hill, at the center of the city's most effective sculptural group of men on horses.
⊞ H5 ⊠ 1st Street NW at the foot of Capitol Hill ⏰ 24 hours 🚇 Capitol South 💵 Free

Grant Memorial below Capitol Hill

HIRSHHORN SCULPTURE GARDEN
In this walled, sunken garden, you are surrounded by works by Henry Moore, Max Ernst, Pablo Picasso, Man Ray and other luminaries.
⊞ H5 ⊠ 7th Street and Jefferson Drive SW ☎ 202/357–2700 ⏰ 7:30AM–dusk 🚇 L'Enfant Plaza 💵 Free

NATIONAL ARBORETUM
The Arboretum's 446 acres invite driving, biking, and hiking. The National Herb Garden and National Bonsai Collection are fascinating, and the Azalea Walk is beautiful in the spring.
⊞ M3–N3 ⊠ 3501 New York Avenue NE ☎ 202/245–2726 ⏰ Daily 8–5 🚇 Brookland–CUA, then bus No. H6 🚌 B2 💵 Free

NATIONAL GALLERY OF ART SCULPTURE GARDEN
Works by Louise Bourgeois, Mark di Suveroi, Roy Lichtenstein, and many other 20th-century artists may be enjoyed in this 6½-acre garden. The reflecting pool becomes a skating rink in winter.
⊞ H5 ⊠ Between Constitution Avenue and the National Mall, 7th and 9th Street NW ☎ 202/737–4215 ⏰ Mon–Sat 10–5; Sun 11–6. Skating rink winter: daily 11AM–10PM 🚇 Archives 💵 Free; skating inexpensive

ROCK CREEK PARK
Washingtonians enjoy 1,800-acre Rock Creek Park for picnicking, biking, hiking, tennis, golf, riding, jogging, and the Nature Center and Planetarium.
⊞ E1–E3 ⊠ Nature Center, 5000 Glover Road NW ☎ 202/426–6829 ⏰ Nature Center Wed–Sun 9–5. Grounds daylight hours 🚇 Woodley Park–Zoo 💵 Free

Korean War Veterans Memorial
Dedicated in 1995, this memorial includes 19 life-size figures marching up an incline toward the American flag, a still pool memorializing those who lost their lives in the war, and photographs of the Korean conflict etched into a 60-foot wall. A memorial of faces, it is a compelling counterpoint to the Vietnam Veterans Memorial wall of names.
⊞ E5 ⊠ Between the Lincoln Memorial and Independence Avenue ☎ 202/208–3561 ⏰ 24 hours 💵 Free

PLACES OF WORSHIP

The D.C. Jewish Community Center

First opened in 1926 and completely redesigned in 1990, the Center at 1529 16th Street NW includes a lap pool, gym with steam rooms, auditorium, classrooms, racquetball courts, library, social hall, gallery, 250-seat theater and kosher restaurant. In essence, almost everything a traveler might need to keep fit in mind and body.

Minaret of the Islamic Mosque and Cultural Center

See Top 25 Sights for
U.S. HOLOCAUST MEMORIAL MUSEUM
(➤ 33)
SHRINE OF THE IMMACULATE CONCEPTION
(➤ 47)

ADAS ISRAEL CONGREGATION

Conservative. Highlights of this post-World War II cast concrete building include a two-story window depicting the Star of David, a ten-foot bronze menorah by Milton Hebald and several sculptures by Phillip Rapner depicting Jewish traditions.

✚ Off map at E1 ✉ 2850 Quebec Street NW ☎ 202/362–4433 ⓠ Cleveland Park

BET MISH PACHAH SYNAGOGUE

Gay and lesbian congregation.

✚ F3 ✉ 16th & Q Streets NW ☎ 202/833–1638 ❓ Services held at D.C. Jewish Community Center ⓠ Dupont Circle

THE IMANI TEMPLE

African-American Catholic congregation founded by Reverend G. Augustus Stalings, Jr. in 1987.

✚ K5 ✉ 609–11 Maryland Avenue NE ☎ 202/388–8155 ⓣ Daily 9–6 ⓠ Union Station

ISLAMIC MOSQUE AND CULTURAL CENTER

Calls to the faithful emanate from a 162-foot minaret here. Inside are Persian carpets, ebony and ivory carvings, stained glass, and mosaics.

✚ E2 ✉ 2551 Massachusetts Avenue NW ☎ 202/332–8343 ⓣ Cultural Center daily 10:30–4:30. For prayer dawn–10:30PM ⓠ Dupont Circle

METROPOLITAN AFRICAN METHODIST EPISCOPAL CHURCH

This redbrick Gothic Revival church, known as the national cathedral of the AME movement, was completed in 1886, paid for by ex-slaves, and built by African-American artisans.

✚ G3 ✉ 1518 M Street NW ☎ 202/331–1426 ⓣ Mon–Sat 10–6 🍴 Home-cooked lunch Thu, Fri 11–2 ⓠ Farragut North

MOUNT ZION HERITAGE CENTER AND METHODIST CHURCH

Established in 1816, this congregation educated black children and adults, created the District's first black library, and served as a stop on the underground railroad which transported Southern slaves to the free North. The church is known for its elaborate pressed-tin ceiling, engravings by African artisans, and embellished cast-iron pillars.

✚ E3 ✉ 1334 29th Street NW ☎ 202/234–0148 ⓣ Easily arranged by appointment ⓠ Dupont Circle

ST. JOHN'S EPISCOPAL CHURCH
Presidents have worshipped in Pew 54 since the church was built by Benjamin Latrobe in a Greek Cross form in 1816. Later additions include a Doric portico and cupola.

✚ F4 ✉ 1525 H Street NW ☎ 202/347–8766 ⏰ Mon–Fri 8–4; Sat 9–3; Sun services 8, 9, 11 Ⓜ McPherson Square

ST. MARY'S EPISCOPAL CHURCH
James Renwick designed this redbrick 1887 Gothic Revival church for D.C.'s first black Protestant Episcopal congregation. The building has a timber roof and French painted-glass windows depicting St. Cyprian and other African religious leaders. A garden offers peace and quiet downtown.

✚ E4 ✉ 728 23rd Street NW ☎ 202/333–3985 ⏰ Daily 9–4 Ⓜ Foggy Bottom

ST. MATTHEW'S CATHEDRAL
President John F. Kennedy's funeral mass was held in this plain Renaissance-style church, the seat of Washington's Catholic archbishop. Inside there are stunning mosaics and gilded Corinthian capitals.

✚ F3 ✉ 1725 Rhode Island Avenue NW ☎ 202/347–3215 ⏰ Sun–Fri 7–6:30; Sat 8–7 Ⓜ Farragut North

TEMPLE MICAH
This intimate post-modern masonry building has great acoustics and a friendly Reform congregation.

✚ D1 ✉ 2829 Wisconsin Avenue ☎ 202/333–4808 Ⓜ Foggy Bottom

WASHINGTON HEBREW CONGREGATION
Reform congregation.

✚ Off map at C1 ✉ 3935 Macomb Street NW ☎ 202/362–7100 Ⓜ Cleveland Park

WASHINGTON NATIONAL CATHEDRAL
On September 30, 1990, President George Bush and thousands of guests watched the placement of the final stone of this Gothic-style building, resplendent with flying buttresses, 518-foot nave, rose window made up of 10,500 pieces of stained glass, stone barrel vaults, and fanciful gargoyles. The stone carving in this, the world's sixth-largest cathedral, is extraordinary. Bring binoculars.

✚ C1–D1 ✉ Wisconsin and Massachusetts Avenues NW ☎ 202/537–6200 ⏰ May–Labor Day: Mon–Fri 10–9; Sat, Sun 10–4:30. Labor Day–Apr: daily 10–4:30 Ⓜ Tenley Town; then 30 series bus south

Quiet places
Do not overlook the Hall of Remembrance in the U.S. Holocaust Memorial Museum. This space invites quiet, nondenominational contemplation, as does Barnett Newman's *14 Stations of the Cross* hanging on the concourse level of the National Gallery of Art.

Washington National Cathedral

VIEWS

See Top 25 Sights for
CEDAR HILL (➤ 48)
**CUSTIS-LEE MANSION AT ARLINGTON
   NATIONAL CEMETERY** (➤ 24)
KENNEDY CENTER ROOF TERRACE (➤ 25)
LIBRARY OF CONGRESS CAFETERIA (➤ 46)
U.S. CAPITOL, WEST FACE (➤ 43)
WASHINGTON MONUMENT (➤ 31)

Francis Scott Key Bridge

The pedestrian-friendly Francis Scott Key Bridge, accessible from M Street in Georgetown, is a great place to see the river or for a view of the Georgetown skyline.

HOTEL WASHINGTON ROOF TERRACE

This national landmark is the oldest continuously operating hotel in the city, known since its opening in 1918 as "the hotel with the view." The terrace overlooks the White House and the Washington Monument, and is *the* place for afternoon tea or sunset cocktails.

➕ G4 ✉ 515 15th Street NW ☎ 202/638–5900 ⏰ Apr 14–Oct 30: daily 11:30AM–1AM 🚇 McPherson Square 💵 Expensive

OLD POST OFFICE BUILDING TOWER

To get your bearings in the city, the clock tower at the Old Post Office has the best view, and the building houses a food court with everything from ice cream to Indian food.

➕ G5 ✉ Pennsylvania Avenue at 12th Street NW ☎ 202/606–8691 ⏰ Easter–Labor Day: daily 8AM–11PM. Labor Day–Mar: daily 10–6 🍴 Many cafés and restaurants 🚇 Federal Triangle 💵 Free

The view from the Old Post Office tower

WASHINGTON
where to...

AMERICAN

Prices

Expect to pay for a meal per person, excluding drinks:

$ up to $20
$$ up to $35
$$$ more than $35

All restaurants mentioned here take major credit cards. It is usually advisable to make a reservation.

AMERICA ($$)

Right in the middle of Union Station, America has all tastes covered with its something-for-everyone menu. Southwest specialties are its strong suit.

🔲 J4 ✉ Union Station, 50 Massachusetts Avenue NE
☎ 202/682–9555 🕐 Daily lunch, dinner Ⓜ Union Station

CASHIONS EAT PLACE ($$)

This Adams-Morgan restaurant serves updated versions of home-style meals. You'll usually find several seafood choices, as well as roast chicken, steak, and lamb. Don't forget to try the buttery mashed potatoes.

🔲 F2 ✉ 1819 Columbia Road NW ☎ 202/797–1819
🕐 Tue–Sat dinner; Sunday brunch Ⓜ Dupont Circle then bus No. L2

CLYDE'S ($–$$)

This longtime fixture in Georgetown (and other locations in the area) is a good bet for basic steak, burgers, and fish.

🔲 D3 ✉ 3236 M Street NW
☎ 202/333–9180 🕐 Daily lunch, dinner; Sat, Sun breakfast Ⓜ Foggy Bottom-GWU then any of bus Nos. 32, 34, 35, 36

GEORGIA BROWN'S ($$)

This elegant restaurant with its conversation nooks is beloved by government officials, lobbyists, and journalists. Pork, lima beans, okra and other Southern specials are delicious here.

🔲 G4 ✉ 950 15th Street NW
☎ 202/393–4499 🕐 Sun–Fri lunch, dinner; Sat dinner Ⓜ McPherson Square

THE MONOCLE ($$$)

This is one of the best restaurants for spotting members of Congress sitting near the fireplaces. Photos of politicians adorn the walls. American food with a Continental touch.

🔲 J5 ✉ 107 D Street NE
☎ 202/546–4488 🕐 Mon–Fri lunch, dinner Ⓜ Union Station

OLD EBBITT GRILL ($$)

One block from the White House, this is one of Washington's busiest restaurants, with an oyster bar, pub food, and family fare.

🔲 G4 ✉ 675 15th Street NW
☎ 202/347–4800 🕐 Daily breakfast, lunch, and dinner
Ⓜ Metro Center

OLD GLORY ($$)

The flags of six big barbecue-eating Southern states hang from the ceiling in this popular updated roadhouse, which serves all variations of barbecued pork, beef, and chicken.

🔲 D3 ✉ 3139 M Street NW
☎ 202/337–3406 🕐 Daily lunch, dinner Ⓜ Foggy Bottom-GWU, then bus Nos. 32, 35, or 38B

B. SMITH'S ($$–$$$)

American cooking with a Southern accent: barbecued ribs, fried catfish and the house specialty, Swamp Thing—mustard-seasoned shrimp and crawfish with collard greens.

🔲 J4 ✉ Union Station, 50 Massachusetts Avenue NE
☎ 202/289–6188 🕐 Daily lunch, dinner Ⓜ Union Station

STEAK & SEAFOOD

GEORGETOWN SEAFOOD GRILL ($$)

You can have the catch-of-the-day prepared one of five ways—grilled, broiled, sautéed, blackened, or poached. Good service.
🚇 D3 ✉ 1200 19th Street NW ☎ 202/530–4430 🕐 Mon–Fri lunch, dinner; Sat, Sun dinner Ⓜ Farragut North

LEGAL SEAFOOD ($$–$$$)

The Boston-based chain now offers Washingtonians up to 40 kinds of fish.
🚇 F4 ✉ 2020 K Street NW ☎ 202/496–1111 🕐 Mon–Fri lunch, dinner; Sat, Sun dinner Ⓜ Farragut West

LES HALLES ($$)

American beef prepared the French way. Cigar smoking upstairs.
🚇 G5 ✉ 1201 Pennsylvania Avenue NW ☎ 202/347–6848 🕐 Daily lunch, dinner Ⓜ Federal Triangle

MORTON'S OF CHICAGO ($$$)

It's not the vinyl-boothed room that draws people here—it's the size and the quality of the steaks. If you're really hungry (or sharing), don't miss the 3-pound porterhouse.
🚇 D3 ✉ 3251 Prospect Street NW ☎ 202/342–6258 🕐 Daily dinner Ⓜ Foggy Bottom, then bus No. 35

THE PALM ($$$)

As plain and business-like as the New York original. In addition to huge steaks, there's a bargain lunch menu of shrimp, veal, and chicken salad.
🚇 F3 ✉ 1225 19th Street NW ☎ 202/293–9091 🕐 Mon–Fri lunch, dinner; Sat, Sun dinner Ⓜ Dupont Circle

PESCE ($$)

Come here to choose from a long list of seafood dishes (changed daily).
🚇 F3 ✉ 2016 P Street NW ☎ 202/466–FISH 🕐 Mon–Sat lunch, dinner; Sun dinner Ⓜ Dupont Circle

PRIME RIB ($$$)

Decorated in black and gold like a 1940s supper club, Prime Rib serves its namesake to the posh meat-and-potatoes set.
🚇 F4 ✉ 2020 K Street NW ☎ 202/466–8811 🕐 Mon–Fri lunch, dinner; Sat dinner Ⓜ Farragut West

RUTH'S CHRIS STEAK HOUSE ($$$)

A branch of the New Orleans-based chain. Offers huge prime-cut steaks, plus lobster, chicken, and veal.
🚇 F3 ✉ 1801 Connecticut Avenue NW ☎ 202/797–0033 🕐 Daily dinner Ⓜ Dupont Circle

SAM & HARRY'S ($$$)

Understated and genteel, this dining room packs them in for porterhouse and strip steaks, prime rib, and daily seafood specials.
🚇 F3 ✉ 1200 19th Street NW ☎ 202/296–4333 🕐 Mon–Fri lunch, dinner; Sat dinner Ⓜ Dupont Circle

SEA CATCH ($$$)

Hidden in a Georgetown courtyard overlooking the C & O Canal, this formal establishment has an outstanding raw bar; offers entrées such as soft-shell crabs sprinkled with diced tomato and pecan halves.
🚇 D3 ✉ 1054 31st Street NW ☎ 202/337–8855 🕐 Mon–Sat lunch, dinner Ⓜ Foggy Bottom, then bus No. 35 or 38B

Seafood southwest

If you have a taste for fish, head down to the southwest waterfront where there is a concentration of seafood restaurants. In Water Street you will find Phillips Flagship; Le Rivage (for French fish dishes); Hogates; Pier Seven; the Gangplank; and, for seafood with a Cajun twist, Creole Orleans.

63

CONTEMPORARY AMERICAN & FRENCH

Quality dining

Long considered a city of mediocre restaurants, Washington has, in recent years, discovered its bounty of regional farm produce and specialties from the sea. Immigrant chefs and their new cuisines have contributed largely to the current dining renaissance. The city has the good fortune to have a chef who was given a two-star rating by the highly regarded *Guide Michelin*: Gérard Pangaud, of Gérard's Place (see main entry, this page).

1789 ($$$)

Housed in a federal town house with a large fireplace, 1789 specializes in innovatively prepared game and seafood.
✚ C3 ✉ 1226 36th Street NW ☎ 202/965–1789 ⏰ Daily dinner Ⓜ Foggy Bottom, then bus No. 32 or 38B

701 RESTAURANT ($$)

This very elegant restaurant, with large windows looking out on Pennsylvania Avenue, offers tapas, a caviar bar, and live jazz every night.
✚ H5 ✉ 701 Pennsylvania Avenue NW ☎ 202/393–0701 ⏰ Mon–Fri lunch, dinner; Sat, Sun dinner Ⓜ Archives

BIS ($$–$$$)

Located in the new Hotel George, Bis offers an extensive wine list to complement appetizers such as snails with artichoke and rabbit galette, and entrées like mussels and duck confit.
✚ J4 ✉ 15 E Street NW ☎ 202/661–2700 ⏰ Daily breakfast, lunch, dinner Ⓜ Union Station

BISTRO FRANCAIS ($$)

Fixed-price lunches and dinner specials are a good deal in this French country restaurant. Stays open well into the night.
✚ D3 ✉ 3128 M Street NW ☎ 202/338–3830 ⏰ Daily lunch, dinner Ⓜ Foggy Bottom, then bus No. 35 or 38B

LA CHAUMIERE ($$$)

Like a rustic French country inn, this restaurant serves French country fare such as *pot-au-feu* and bouillabaisse.
✚ E3 ✉ 2813 M Street NW ☎ 202/338–1784 ⏰ Mon–Fri lunch, dinner; Sat dinner Ⓜ Foggy Bottom

CITIES ($$)

Follow your duck confit on a crispy potato pancake with entrées like halibut with leeks or mixed grill. The front dining area resembles a service station.
✚ F2 ✉ 2424 18th Street NW ☎ 202/328–7194 ⏰ Mon–Sat dinner Ⓜ Dupont Circle, then bus No. 42

CITRONELLE AT THE LATHAM HOTEL ($$$)

Consistently among Washington's top restaurants for its creative contemporary food.
✚ D3 ✉ Latham Hotel, 3000 M Street NW ☎ 202/625–2150 ⏰ Daily breakfast, lunch, dinner Ⓜ Foggy Bottom, then bus No. 35 or 38B

LA COLLINE ($$)

Seafood—fricassée, grilled or gratinée—is one measure of this consistently excellent Capitol Hill favorite.
✚ J5 ✉ 400 N Capitol Street NW ☎ 202/737–0400 ⏰ Mon–Fri breakfast, lunch, dinner; Sat dinner Ⓜ Union Station

DC COAST ($$)

Appetizers include osso buco, veal ravioli, and Virginia smoked trout salad. Follow that with Chinese style smoked lobster with crispy spinach or grilled Angus ribeye with green chili macaroni and cheese.
✚ G4 ✉ 1401 K Street NW ☎ 202/216–5988 ⏰ Mon–Fri lunch, dinner; Sat dinner Ⓜ McPherson Square

LA FOURCHETTE ($$)

A bit of Paris in Adams-Morgan, with tin ceiling, bentwood chairs, quasi-Post-Impressionist murals, and sturdy bistro cuisine such as veal or lamb shanks.
✚ F2 ✉ 2429 18th Street NW ☎ 202/332–3077 🕐 Mon–Fri lunch; daily dinner 🚇 Woodley Park–Zoo then bus Nos. 90, 91, 92, 93 or 96

GÉRARD'S PLACE ($$$)

Gérard Pangaud takes New American fare to greater heights; try the seared tuna.
✚ G4 ✉ 915 15th Street NW ☎ 202/737–4445 🕐 Mon–Fri lunch, dinner; Sat dinner 🚇 McPherson Square

KINKEAD'S ($$–$$$)

One of D.C.'s best restaurants, Kinkead's is an updated seafood restaurant, with seafood ravioli, grilled squid, and pepita-encrusted salmon.
✚ F4 ✉ 2000 Pennsylvania Avenue NW ☎ 202/296–7700 🕐 Daily lunch, dinner 🚇 Foggy Bottom

LESPINASSE ($$$)

Lespinasse is possibly Washington's best French restaurant. Try Chef Sandro Gamba's seared rockfish fillet with shaved black truffle or lacquered supreme of squab with confit of garlic. In the Sheraton Carlton Hotel.
✚ F4 ✉ 923 16th Street NW ☎ 202/879–6900 🕐 Daily lunch; Tue–Sat dinner 🚇 Farragut North

NEW HEIGHTS ($$)

Attractive. Includes appetizers such as foie gras with mango salsa and entrées such as spiced lamb chops and filet mignon with pickled fennel and blue cheese.
✚ E1 ✉ 2317 Calvert Street NW ☎ 202/234–4110 🕐 Mon–Sat dinner 🚇 Woodley Park–Zoo

NORA ($$$)

The menu changes daily in this restaurant full of exposed brick and decorated with quilts. Organic vegetables and free-range meats come in unusual combinations.
✚ E3 ✉ 2132 Florida Avenue NW ☎ 202/462–5143 🕐 Mon–Sat dinner 🚇 Dupont Circle

OCCIDENTAL GRILL ($$–$$$)

The photo-covered walls suggest an old Washington club, but the menu is far from conservative with its grill and marinated tuna.
✚ G4 ✉ 1475 Pennsylvania Avenue NW ☎ 202/783–1475 🕐 Daily lunch, dinner 🚇 Metro Center

TABARD INN ($$)

With its parlor-like dining rooms and lovely outdoor terrace, the Tabard is a pleasure for its organic vegetables and hormone-free beef.
✚ F3 ✉ 1739 N Street NW ☎ 202/ 833–2668 🕐 Daily breakfast, lunch, dinner 🚇 Dupont Circle

TWO QUAIL ($$$)

On Capitol Hill, this cozy, stuffed-with-curios dining room offers American-inspired food such as pork chops and apple pie.
✚ J5 ✉ 320 Massachusetts Avenue NE ☎ 202/543–8030 🕐 Mon–Fri lunch; daily dinner 🚇 Union Station

Hotel restaurants

Some of Washington's best restaurants are in the finer hotels, with creative, contemporary fare drawing on the best American ingredients and classic French cooking techniques. Try Citronelle in the Latham (➤ 85), the Jefferson Hotel restaurant (202/347–2200 in Georgetown), the dining room in the Morrison-Clark Inn (➤ 85), and Lafayette at the Hay-Adams (➤ 84). Though all tend toward the expensive, food and service are generally first-rate.

65

ITALIAN

Door-to-door dining

If you find yourself hungry in your hotel room, but don't want room service food, try one of several pizza delivery services. Domino's is the largest chain, with many locations. Pizza Hut has a few delivery outlets. Armand's ☎ 202/547–6600 on Capitol Hill or 202/363–5500 for upper Wisconsin Avenue; Geppetto ☎ 202/333–4315, in Georgetown, and Trio Pizza ☎ 202/232–5611, near Dupont Circle, all deliver.

CAFÉ MILANO ($$$)

Fettuccine, Bolognese, risottos and grilled fish are the specialties in this favorite Georgetown gathering place.

✚ E3 ✉ 3251 Prospect Street NW ☎ 202/333–6183 ◉ Daily lunch, dinner ⓠ Foggy Bottom, then bus No. 36 or 38B

GALILEO ($$$)

Twice daily Galileo changes its menu using homemade items from bread-sticks to mozzarella, and Italian specialties of grilled fish, game birds, and veal. Extensive wine list.

✚ F4 ✉ 1110 21st Street NW ☎ 202/293–7191 ◉ Mon–Fri breakfast, lunch, dinner; Sat, Sun dinner ⓠ Foggy Bottom

I MATTI ($$)

The less-expensive sister restaurant to Galileo above. The extensive menu ranges from pizza to homey polenta, with lots of daily dinner specials, such as rabbit.

✚ F2 ✉ 2436 18th Street NW ☎ 202/462–8844 ◉ Tue–Sat lunch, dinner; Sun dinner ⓠ Woodley Park–Zoo

OTELLO ($)

In this quaint spot you'll find inexpensive, simply prepared meat and fish dishes such as red snapper with capers and olives.

✚ F3 ✉ 1329 Connecticut Avenue NW ☎ 202/429–0209 ◉ Mon–Fri lunch, dinner; Sat dinner ⓠ Dupont Circle

PIZZERIA PARADISO ($)

This pizzeria, with a trompe l'œil ceiling, serves deliciously fresh versions of the basics: pizzas, salads, sandwiches.

✚ F3 ✉ 2029 P Street NW ☎ 202/223–1245 ◉ Daily lunch, dinner ⓠ Dupont Circle

PRIMI PIATTI ($$$)

House specialties include pastas, antipasti and grilled items made with quality ingredients. Outdoor dining in summer.

✚ F4 ✉ 2013 I Street NW ☎ 202/223–3600 ◉ Mon–Fri lunch, dinner; Sat dinner ⓠ Farragut West

IL RADICCHIO ($–$$)

You can get pizza cooked in a wood-burning oven or sandwiches, but the main attraction here is the all-you-can-eat spaghetti.

✚ F3 ✉ 1509 17th Street NW ☎ 202/986–2627 ◉ Mon–Sat lunch, dinner; Sun dinner ⓠ Dupont Circle

✚ D3 ✉ 1211 Wisconsin Avenue NW ☎ 202/ 337–2627 ⓠ Foggy Bottom, then bus No. 32, or 38B

✚ J6 ✉ 223 Pennsylvania Avenue SE ☎ 202/547–5114 ⓠ Capitol South

I RICCHI ($$$)

This airy Tuscan dining room, with terra-cotta tiles and floral frescoes, serves spit-roasted meats and a seasonal menu, and attracts the business crowd.

✚ F3 ✉ 1220 19th Street NW ☎ 202/835–0459 ◉ Mon–Fri lunch, dinner; Sat dinner ⓠ Dupont Circle

LA TOMATE ($$$)

Homemade pastas and smoked fish with a pianist adding to the romance.

✚ F3 ✉ 1701 Connecticut Avenue NW ☎ 202/667–5505 ◉ Daily lunch, dinner ⓠ Dupont Circle

Spanish, Latin & Tex-Mex

AUSTIN GRILL ($)
Adobe pastels and Texas
music draw a young crowd
for sizzling chicken, steak
fajitas, and chips with
salsa.
➕ C2 ✉ 2404 Wisconsin Avenue
NW ☎ 202/337–8080 ⏰ Daily
lunch, dinner Ⓜ Foggy Bottom,
then bus No. 32 or 34

CAFÉ ATLANTICO ($–$$$)
Lovely Caribbean food—
look for appetizers like
tuna *ceviche* and soft shell
crabs in passion fruit, and
entrées such as salmon
with papaya, and *feijoada*,
the Brazilian meat stew
made with black beans
flavored with pork and
smoked meat.
➕ H5 ✉ 405 8th Street NW
☎ 202/393–0812 ⏰ Mon–Sat
lunch; daily dinner
Ⓜ Archives/Navy Memorial

COCO LOCO ($$$)
Two restaurants in one—a
tapas bar and a Brazilian
churrasqueria, where grilled
meat is brought to your
table and sliced on your
plate. On Thursday to
Saturday nights, half the
area becomes a night club.
➕ H4 ✉ 810 7th Street NW
☎ 202/289–2626 ⏰ Mon–Fri
lunch; daily dinner Ⓜ Gallery
Place–Chinatown

THE GRILL FROM IPANEMA ($$)
The Brazilian menu at this
Adams-Morgan restaurant
ranges from spicy sea-
food stews to traditional
feijoada (served Wednesday
and Saturday).
➕ F2 ✉ 1858 Columbia Road NW
☎ 202/986–0757 ⏰ Mon–Fri
dinner; Sat, Sun lunch, dinner
Ⓜ Woodley Park–Zoo then walk
nine blocks or bus No. 90, 99, or L2

JALEO ($$)
Hot and cold tapas are the
house specialty.
➕ H5 ✉ 480 7th Street NW
☎ 202/628–7949 ⏰ Daily
lunch and dinner Ⓜ Archives–Navy
Memorial

LAURIOL PLAZA ($$)
Simple, Spanish/South
American restaurant,
whose specialties include
mesquite wood- and
charcoal-grilled meats and
vegetables, and freshly
made tortillas and nachos.
➕ F2 ✉ 1835 18th Street NW
☎ 202/387–0035 ⏰ Daily
lunch, dinner Ⓜ Dupont Circle

PEYOTE CAFÉ ($)
Pub serving standard Tex-
Mex items and vegetarian
dishes. Located below
Roxanne; you may order
their Southwestern menu.
➕ F2 ✉ 2319 18th Street NW
☎ 202/462–8330 ⏰ Mon–Fri
dinner; Sat, Sun lunch, dinner
Ⓜ Woodley Park–Zoo then walk
seven blocks, or bus No. 99 or L2

RED SAGE ($$$)
In this faux-adobe warren
of dining rooms, peppers
are in everything but
desserts, and portions and
prices are big. There is a
chili bar and café upstairs.
➕ G4 ✉ 605 14th Street NW
☎ 202/638–4444 ⏰ Mon–Fri
lunch; daily dinner Ⓜ Metro Center

TABERNA DEL ALABARDERO ($$$)
Attentive service and plush
decor create a romantic
setting for tapas and
seafood paella.
➕ F4 ✉ 1776 I Street NW
(entrance on 18th Street) ☎ 202/
429–2200 ⏰ Mon–Fri lunch,
dinner; Sat dinner Ⓜ Farragut West

Bethesda feasting
Bethesda, just across the District
line in Maryland, has in the past
few years become a veritable
city of restaurants. A walk along
a two-block stretch of Cordell
Avenue provides several
different international dining
options: Cesco Trattoria (Italian
✉ 4871 Cordell Avenue
☎ 301/654–8333; Cottonwood
Café (Southwestern American
✉ 4844 Cordell Avenue
☎ 301/656–4844); Faryab
(Afghan ✉ 4917 Cordell
Avenue ☎ 301/951–3484);
Matuba (Japanese ✉ 4918
Cordell Avenue ☎ 301/652–
7449) and Oodles Noodles
(Asian ✉ 4907 Cordell Avenue
☎ 301/986–8833).

PAN-ASIAN

Chinatown

Washington's Chinatown, several somewhat run-down blocks around 7th and H Streets NW, has some good restaurants, including Hunan Chinatown ✉ 624 H Street NW; Mr Yung's ✉ 740 6th Street NW; China Inn ✉ 631 H Street NW; Tony Cheng's Mongolian Restaurant ✉ 619 H Street NW, and Full Kee ✉ 509 H Street NW. A few other ethnic restaurants are here as well, including Burma (see main entry this page).

Budget meals

Downtown in the area bounded by Pennsylvania Avenue, M Street, 14th Street, and 21st Street there are many places where you can get soup, a sandwich, and salad on a tight budget. Most of these spots cater to office workers and are open only on weekdays for breakfast and lunch. The chain Au Bon Pain has many locations around town, including 1801 L Street NW, 1401 I Street NW, 1850 M Street NW, and 706 L'Enfant Plaza SW.

BENKAY ($$)
The main attraction here is the buffet of sushi, tempura, and other Japanese fare.
🚇 G4 ✉ 727 15th Street NW, lower level ☎ 202/737–1515 🕐 Mon–Fri lunch 🚇 McPherson Square

BURMA ($)
A Chinatown alternative to Chinese food. The Burmese specialties include mango pork and tamarind fish. Start your meal with batter-dipped fried eggplant or squash, with spicy dips.
🚇 H4 ✉ 740 6th Street NW ☎ 202/638–1280 🕐 Mon–Fri lunch; daily dinner 🚇 Gallery Place/Chinatown

BUSARA ($$)
This Thai restaurant, stylish in black rubber, brushed steel, and lacquer, stands out for its unusual red curry duck and cellophane noodles with three kinds of mushroom.
🚇 C2 ✉ 2340 Wisconsin Avenue NW ☎ 202/337–2340 🕐 Daily lunch, dinner 🚇 Foggy Bottom, then bus No. 34 or 36

CAFÉ ASIA ($)
There are few staff, but low prices and the choice of cuisines —Singaporean, Indonesian, Japanese, Thai, Chinese, and Vietnamese— make the wait at this spartan eatery worthwhile.
🚇 F3 ✉ 1134 19th Street NW ☎ 202/659–2696 🕐 Mon–Sat lunch, dinner; Sun dinner 🚇 Dupont Circle

CITY LIGHTS OF CHINA ($$)
The surroundings are basic, but the food is top shelf. Known for its steamed dumplings, Singapore rice noodles, crispy shredded beef, and Hunan chicken.
🚇 F3 ✉ 1731 Connecticut Avenue NW ☎ 202/265–6688 🕐 Daily lunch, dinner 🚇 Dupont Circle

LITTLE VIET GARDEN ($)
One of the many Vietnamese restaurants in Arlington, with terrace dining in season. Another good bet nearby: Queen Bee (✉ 3181 Wilson Boulevard ☎ 703/527–3444).
🚇 A5 ✉ 3012 Wilson Boulevard, Arlington, VA ☎ 703/522–9686 🕐 Daily lunch, dinner 🚇 Clarendon

SAIGON GOURMET ($$)
Service is brisk and friendly at this popular, Vietnamese dining room; try the grilled pork with rice crêpes.
🚇 E1 ✉ 2635 Connecticut Avenue NW ☎ 202/265–1360 🕐 Daily lunch, dinner 🚇 Woodley Park–Zoo

SALA THAI ($$)
Mirrored walls and soft lights soften this small Thai restaurant serving good noodles and curries.
🚇 F3 ✉ 2016 P Street NW ☎ 202/872–1144 🕐 Daily lunch, dinner 🚇 Dupont Circle

STRAITS OF MALAYA ($–$$)
Malaysian food seems like a mix of Chinese, Indian and Thai foods. *Poh pia* is reminiscent of *mu shu*, but without the pork. Noodle dishes, curries, and Indonesian fried rice round out the menu.
🚇 F2 ✉ 1836 18th Street NW ☎ 202/483–1483 🕐 Mon–Fri lunch; daily dinner 🚇 Dupont Circle

INDIAN, AFRICAN & MIDDLE EASTERN

AATISH ON THE HILL ($–$$)

Choose from a variety of tandoori, biryani, and other Pakistani dishes, or try the house specialty, shahi korma: chunks of lamb in a sauce of yogurt and spices.
✚ K6 ⊠ 609 Pennsylvania Avenue SE ☎ 202/544–0931 ⊕ Mon–Sat lunch, dinner; Sun dinner 🄰 Eastern Market

ADITI ($)

This elegant Indian restaurant, with burgundy carpets and chairs, and pale mint-colored walls with brass sconces, serves lovely breads and curries. The second floor overlooks Georgetown's M Street.
✚ D3 ⊠ 3299 M Street NW ☎ 202/625–6825 ⊕ Daily lunch, dinner 🄰 Foggy Bottom, then bus No. 35, 38B

BACCHUS ($$)

An intimate Lebanese restaurant in a basement; put together a meal from the long list of appetizers.
✚ F3 ⊠ 1827 Jefferson Place NW ☎ 202/785–0734 ⊕ Mon–Fri lunch, dinner; Sat dinner 🄰 Dupont Circle

THE BOMBAY CLUB ($$–$$$)

A block from the White House, this beautiful Indian restaurant, with its potted palms and a bright blue ceiling edged with white plaster moldings, emulates a private British club in 19th-century India. The breads are first-rate, and the seafood dishes, such as lobster Malabar, are superb.
✚ F4 ⊠ 815 Connecticut Avenue NW ☎ 202/659–3727 ⊕ Daily dinner; Mon–Fri lunch; Sun brunch 🄰 Farragut West

BUKOM CAFÉ ($)

Sunny African pop music, and a spicy West African menu filled with goat, lamb, chicken, and vegetable entrées brighten this narrow two-story dining room decked out with potted palms and kente cloth. There is live music nightly, and the kitchen stays open late.
✚ F2 ⊠ 2442 18th Street NW ☎ 202/265–4600 ⊕ Tue–Sun dinner 🄰 Woodley Park–Zoo, then bus No. 92 or 96

MARRAKESH ($$)

In this Moroccan restaurant, on a block of auto repair and supply shops, you share a fixed-price feast with everyone at your table and eat without cutlery. Belly dancers put on nightly shows.
✚ H4 ⊠ 617 New York Avenue NW ☎ 202/393–9393 ⊕ Daily dinner 🄰 Gallery Place–Chinatown

SKEWERS ($)

Kebabs are the specialty of this Middle Eastern restaurant—meat, vegetable or shrimp—served with almond-flecked rice or pasta.
✚ F3 ⊠ 1633 P Street NW ☎ 202/387–7400 ⊕ Daily lunch, dinner 🄰 Dupont Circle

ZED'S ETHIOPIAN CUISINE ($)

This simple Georgetown outpost beguiles you with its tangy *njera*: a bubbly bread that you can dip into the spicy meat and vegetable stews.
✚ E3 ⊠ 1201 28th Street NW ☎ 202/333–4710 ⊕ Daily lunch, dinner 🄰 Foggy Bottom, then bus No. 35

Adams-Morgan eating

Adams-Morgan, the city's most multi-culturally diverse neighborhood, is crowded, bustling, and filled with ethnic restaurants. A walk along 18th Street leads past Saigonnais (Vietnamese ⊠ 2307 18th Street), Meskerem (Ethiopian ⊠ 2434 18th Street), Montego Café (Jamaican ⊠ 2437 18th Street), the Star of Siam (Vietnamese ⊠ 2446 18th Street), and Fasika's (Ethiopian ⊠ 2447 18th Street).

SHOPPING DISTRICTS, MALLS & DEPARTMENT STORES

Opening hours

Stores stay open from Monday to Saturday between 10 and 7 (or 8). Some have extended hours on Thursday while those in shopping or tourist areas are often open on Sunday from 10 or noon until 5 or 6.

ADAMS-MORGAN

Bohemian, eccentric, multicultural Adams-Morgan, within three blocks of 18th Street NW and Columbia Road, has some truly unusual shopping. Look for Afro-centric apparel and accessories, Haitian art, hand-crafted jewelry, 1950s relics and Skynear and Company (✉ 1800 Wyoming Avenue NW ☎ 202/797–7160), the most upscale eclectic home decorating shop in the city.

CHEVY CHASE PAVILION

The Pavilion, a conservatory-style building near the Mazza Galerie, houses such stores as Country Road Australia, Joan Van, and Gazelle Wearable Art, among others. The mall's Canyon Café, Cheesecake Factory, California Pizza Kitchen, and Mozzarella's compete with the usual mall food court.
✚ Off map at C1 ✉ 5335 Wisconsin Avenue NW ☎ 202/686–5335 🕐 Mon–Fri 10–8; Sat 10–6; Sun noon–5 🚇 Friendship Heights

CITY PLACE MALL

For discounted brands look at Nordstrom Rack, Ross, Marshall's, Shoe Rack, Nine West, and four dozen other retailers. Kick back afterward at the movies (10 screens) or grab a bite at the food court.
✚ Off map at H1 ✉ 8661 Colesville Road, Silver Spring MD ☎ 301/589–1091 🕐 Mon–Sat 10–9; Sun noon–6 🚇 Silver Spring

CONNECTICUT AVENUE

North of Dupont Circle, Connecticut Avenue provides a lively mix of restaurants and stores. Look for modern furniture, housewares, shoes, and coffee bars, and bookstores. South of the circle, Connecticut is home to upscale department stores and boutiques, especially for women.
✚ E1–F4

EASTERN MARKET

Gentrified Capitol Hill retains the Eastern Market, where you'll find fresh food on Saturdays and an antiques and imports bazaar on Sundays. Surrounding the market are antiques stores and secondhand clothing stores. Coffee bars sell restorative drinks and grilled vegetable sandwiches. For breakfast or lunch, don't overlook the venerable Market Lunch, which serves old-style ham and eggs, enormous flapjacks with rich blueberry topping, and the city's best crab cakes.
✚ K6 ✉ Pennsylvania Avenue and 7th Street SE 🕐 Tue–Sat 7–6; Sun 9–4 🚇 Eastern Market

FASHION CENTER

Macy's and Nordstrom anchor the 160 shops in this Pentagon City mall. Nordstrom's clerks are superbly trained to assist you, whether you are browsing or buying a fur coat. Across the street you'll find Borders Books and Music and several discount housewares and clothing outlets.

✚ D8 ✉ 1100 S Hayes Street at Army-Navy Drive and I-395 S ☎ 703/415–2400 🕐 Mon–Sat 10–9:30; Sun 11–6 Ⓜ Pentagon City

GEORGETOWN PARK

The upscale spacious, three-level mall is a delight for anyone heading to Wisconsin and M, the heart of George-town shopping. Many galleries, antiques stores, and boutiques are within an easy walk. The crowd is young and hip; apparel and decorator shops are as tasteful as they are pricey.
✚ D3 ✉ 3222 M Street NW ☎ 202/298–5577 🕐 Mon–Sat 10–9; Sun noon–6 Ⓜ Foggy Bottom, then bus No. 35 or 38B

HECHT AND COMPANY

Hecht's, the major local department store, is well laid out and diverse, so you can find everything from the conservative to the trendy.
✚ G4 ✉ 12th and G Streets NW ☎ 202/628–6661 🕐 Daily 10–8 Ⓜ Metro Center

MAZZA GALLERIE

This fancy mall is anchored by ritzy Neiman Marcus; there's also a discount Filene's Basement (with 40 other shops offering cookware including Williams-Sonoma and Laura Ashley Home); good women's shoes (Stephane Kélian); maternity wear for the fashion conscious (Pea in the Pod); and one-of-a-kind furnishings and gifts with a southwestern flavor (Skynear and Company).

✚ Off map at C1 ✉ 5300 Wisconsin Avenue NW ☎ 202/966–6114 🕐 Mon–Fri 10–8; Sat 10–6; Sun noon–5 Ⓜ Friendship Heights

POTOMAC MILLS MALL

This big deal of outlet malls is now Virginia's largest tourist attraction, with retailers such as Ikea, J.C. Penney, and Marshall's, 15 movie theaters, and a food court offering everything from ice cream to sushi.
✚ Off map at B10 ✉ 3900 Potomac Mills Circle, Prince William, VA (30 miles south of D.C. off I-95) ☎ 703/643–1770 🕐 Daily 11–8

SHOPS AT NATIONAL PLACE

Useful to know about because it's well located in the National Press Club. Keep your eyes peeled for local celebrities as you shop in Sharper Image, Banana Republic, and Victoria's Secret.
✚ G4 ✉ F Street NW between 13th and 14th ☎ 202/662–1250 Ⓜ Metro Center

UNION STATION

The city's main railway station also doubles up as one of the U.S.'s largest shopping malls where you can wander along marble-floored avenues under vaulted ceilings. Good for gifts and souvenirs.
✚ J4 ✉ 50 Massachusetts Avenue, NE ☎ 202/371–9441 🕐 Mon–Sat 10–9; Sun noon–6 Ⓜ Union Station

Stay cool

Washington summers are only bearable because of air conditioning, and the malls crank up the coolers to accommodate shoppers, diners, and movie-goers. So when the heat gets to you, it may be time to "shop til you drop".

CLOTHING

Understated elegance

Washingtonians cultivate a studied casualness, but high-fashion shopping is plentiful in addition to the upscale stores in the Watergate and Willard hotels. If you want office or tourist attire, you can get great buys almost everywhere.

BRITCHES OF GEORGETOWN
Stylish men come to these two stores for smart traditional clothing.
✚ F4 ✉ 1776 K Street NW
☎ 202/347–8994 ⏰ Mon–Fri 10–7; Sat 10–6 🚇 Farragut North or West
✚ D3 ✉ 1247 Wisconsin Avenue NW ☎ 202/338–3330
⏰ Mon–Fri 10–7; Sat 10–6; Sun noon–6 🚇 Foggy Bottom, then bus No. 35 or 38B

BROOKS BROTHERS
A real institution (founded 1818), the U.S.'s oldest men's specialty store.
✚ F4 ✉ 1201 Connecticut Avenue ☎ 202/659–4650
⏰ Mon–Fri 9:30–7; Sat 9:30–6; Sun noon–5 🚇 Farragut North

BURBERRYS
The store that introduced Americans to the trenchcoat also sells other fine traditional, apparel.
✚ F3 ✉ 1155 Connecticut Avenue NW ☎ 202/463–3000
⏰ Mon–Fri 9:30–7; Sat 9:30–6; Sun noon–5 🚇 Dupont Circle, Farragut North

CHANEL
Chanel's third largest store in America is in the Willard Hotel, full of pricey, desirable women's clothes and accessories.
✚ G4 ✉ 1455 Pennsylvania Avenue, NW ☎ 202/638–5055
⏰ Mon–Sat 10–6 🚇 Metro Center

FORECAST
Well-known for their excellent service and for their classic, stylish clothing for women.
✚ K6 ✉ 218 7th Street SE
☎ 202/547–7337 ⏰ Tue–Fri 11–7; Sat 10–6; Sun noon–5 🚇 Eastern Market

HECHT'S
Downtown's only remaining department store. Contemporary brands for men, women, and children.
✚ G4 ✉ 12th & G Streets NW
☎ 202/628–6661 ⏰ Mon–Sat 10–8; Sun noon–6 🚇 Metro Center

J. PRESS
The Ivy League look since 1902.
✚ F4 ✉ 1801 L Street NW
☎ 202/857–0120 ⏰ Mon–Sat 9:30–6 🚇 Farragut West

KHISMET WEARABLE ART
Unusual and beautiful designs for men and women in African fabrics.
✚ F2 ✉ 1800 Belmont Road NW
☎ 202/234–7778 ⏰ Sat 1–8; Sun 1–6, or by appointment
🚇 Dupont Circle

KOBOS
West African clothing, accessories, and African music.
✚ F2 ✉ 2444 18th Street NW
☎ 202/332–9580 ⏰ Mon–Sat 11–8 🚇 Dupont Circle

RIZIK BROTHERS
A locally famous ladies' outfitters, known for designer clothing and expert service.
✚ F3 ✉ 1100 Connecticut Avenue NW ☎ 202/223–4050
⏰ Mon–Sat 9–6; Thu until 8
🚇 Farragut North

TOAST & STRAWBERRIES
Original clothing from around the world, plus art work and art wear.
✚ F3 ✉ 1608 20th Street NW
☎ 202/234–1212 ⏰ Mon–Sat 11–7; Sun 1–6 🚇 Dupont Circle

MARKETS & SPECIALTY FOODSTORES

DEAN & DELUCA

Occupying one of the 19th-century farmers' markets on Georgetown's main street, this New York export offers thousands of lovely products, from bakery goods and double-fat cheese to designer vegetables, salads, and elegant entrées, coffee and pastries.

D3 ⊠ 3276 M Street NW ☎ 202/342–2500 🕐 Sun–Thu 10–8; Fri, Sat 10–9 🚇 Foggy Bottom, then bus No. 38B

EASTERN MARKET

The source of the freshest produce in Washington (➤ 70).

K6 ⊠ 7th and C Streets SE ☎ 202/546–2698 🕐 Tue–Sat 7–6; Sun 9–4 🚇 Eastern Market

THE FRENCH MARKET

This market continues to educate the local palate with home-made pâtés, escargots, baguettes, croissants, and French cheeses.

D2 ⊠ 1626–32 Wisconsin Avenue NW ☎ 202/338–4828 🕐 Tue–Sat 8:30–6 🚇 Tenley Town

FRESH FIELDS WHOLE FOODS MARKET

Look to this outlet of the small national chain for wonderful, mostly organic foods and old-fashioned customer service. There's delicious bread, and a gourmet delicatessen, while the oatmeal cookies with maple sugar icing can't be beaten.

Off map at C1 ⊠ 4530 40th Street NW ☎ 202/237–5800 🕐 Mon–Sat 8AM–10PM; Sun 8–8 🚇 Tenley Town

A LITTERI

Situated in the heart of the wholesale food market since 1932, this Italian old-timer is worth the short cab ride from downtown. You'll find more than 40 olive oils and wines to go with every pasta dish you can dream up.

K3 ⊠ 517 Morse Street NE ☎ 202/544–0183 🕐 Tue, Wed 8–4; Thu, Fri 8–5; Sat 8–3 🚇 Union Station, then bus No. D8 or take a cab

LAWSON'S

Single professionals come here for salads, prepared entrées, wines, and baked goodies.

F3 ⊠ 1350 Connecticut Avenue NW ☎ 202/775–0400 🕐 Mon–Fri 7:30AM–8PM; Sat 10–6 🚇 Dupont Circle

RED SAGE GENERAL STORE

An outgrowth of the popular southwestern restaurant next door, this store sells chili peppers and hot-hot-hot to mild salsa, fancy olive oils, herbal vinegars, fresh-baked breads and desserts.

G4 ⊠ 14th and F Streets NW ☎ 202/638–3276 🕐 Mon–Fri 8–3 🚇 Metro Center

UPTOWN BAKERS

A favorite amongst many Washingtonians for its wonderful bakery products; you can also buy take-away soups and sandwiches here.

Off map at E1 ⊠ 3313 Connecticut Avenue NW ☎ 202/362–6262 🕐 Mon–Sat 7AM–7:30PM; Sun 7:30–7 🚇 Cleveland Park

Shopping in style

Washington is a city for gourmets and it's hard to resist the high-quality foods on offer in specialist shops. The atmosphere in the markets makes shopping fun, especially when prices are often lower than in supermarkets.

ANTIQUES, CRAFTS & GIFTS

Treasure-hunting

Georgetown, Adams-Morgan, Dupont Circle, and the 7th Street art corridor are abundantly supplied with galleries, boutiques, and specialty stores.

Museum shops

No serious shopper should overlook them. In addition to books geared to a museum's topic you'll find reproduction furnishings and decorative arts, jewelry, and apparel related to the museum's collection. The Smithsonian is Washington's third-largest retailer. The Hirshhorn Museum offers modern jewelry; the National Museum of American History has reproduction 19th-century toys, kitchenware, and quilts; the Corcoran offers blown-glass objects and woven scarves; the Building Museum sells tools and architectural puzzles. Look for Alphabets and cartoon animation in the National Children's Museum, bonsai pots in the National Arboretum, the latest stamps at the National Postal Museum, and freeze-dried ice cream at the National Air and Space Museum.

AMBIANCE GALLERIES
These well-appointed galleries place emphasis on one-of-a-kind accessories, including sculpture, fine art, porcelain, furniture, and lighting.
✚ D3 ✉ 1647 Wisconsin Avenue NW ☎ 202/944–4007 ⏰ Mon–Sat 11–5 Ⓜ Foggy Bottom, then bus No. 34

THE AMERICAN HAND
This gallery-shop sells one-of-a-kind and limited-edition international ceramics, textiles, and wood crafts for home and office.
✚ E3 ✉ 2906 M Street NW ☎ 202/965–3273 ⏰ Mon–Sat 11–6; Sun 1–5 Ⓜ Farragut West, then bus No. 32

APPALACHIAN SPRING
Seek this out for ceramics, quilts, fine woodwork, and other traditional and contemporary crafts.
✚ D3 ✉ 1415 Wisconsin Avenue NW ☎ 202/337–5780 ⏰ Mon–Sat 10–9; Sun noon–5 Ⓜ Farragut West, then bus No. 32

CANAL SQUARE GALLERIES
Specialties include central and eastern European art, contemporary Asian artists, and modern realism in these three separate galleries under one roof.
✚ D3 ✉ 3112 M Street NW ☎ 202/338–6456 ⏰ Tue–Sat noon–6 Ⓜ Foggy Bottom, then bus No. 34

CHENONCEAU ANTIQUES
American 19th- and 20th-century antiques, and

mission oak are chosen here by someone with a sophisticated knowledge of this period.
✚ F2 ✉ 2314 18th Street NW ☎ 202/667–1651 ⏰ Sat, Sun noon–6:30 Ⓜ Dupont Circle, then bus No. 42

CHERISHABLES
The emphasis here is on 18th-century Federal furniture and decorations.
✚ F3 ✉ 1608 20th Street NW ☎ 202/785–4087 ⏰ Mon–Sat 11–6 Ⓜ Dupont Circle

DISCOVERY CHANNEL STORE
Four-level store selling unique products from around the world designed to educate and entertain.
✚ H4 ✉ MCI Center, 601 F Street NW ☎ 202/639–0908 ⏰ Mon–Sat 10–7; Sun noon–6 Ⓜ Gallery Place–Chinatown

GALLERIES OF DUPONT CIRCLE
Fine contemporary and older art from around the world are on offer in these 22 independent galleries.
✚ F3 ✉ 1710 Connecticut Avenue NW ☎ 202/328–7189 ⏰ Tue–Sat 11–5 Ⓜ Dupont Circle

GEORGETOWN ANTIQUES CENTER
Victorian art nouveau and art deco objects are displayed in an accommodating Victorian townhouse.
✚ E3 ✉ 2918 M Street NW ☎ 202/338–3811 ⏰ Mon–Sat 11–6; Sun noon–5 Ⓜ Foggy Bottom

G.K.S. BUSH
Browse among early American high-style furniture and related art.

✚ E3 ✉ 2828 Pennsylvania Avenue NW ☎ 202/965–0653 🕐 Mon–Fri 10–6; Sat 10–5 🚇 Foggy Bottom

INDIAN CRAFT SHOP

This shop showcases hand-crafted Eskimo walrus-ivory carving, Zuni pots, Hopi dolls, and Navajo pottery.

✚ F5 ✉ Department of Interior, 1849 C Street NW, Room 1023 ☎ 202/208–4056 🕐 Mon–Fri 8:30–4:30 🚇 Farragut West

KEITH LIPERT GALLERY

American and European decorative art from contemporary designers.

✚ E3 ✉ 2922 M Street NW ☎ 202/965–9736 🕐 Mon–Sat 11–6; Sun 1–5 🚇 Foggy Bottom

MARSTON LUCE

American folk art, weather-vanes, and geometric textiles line the shelves.

✚ F5 ✉ 1314 21st Street NW ☎ 202/775–9460 🕐 Mon–Sat 11–6 🚇 Farragut West, then bus No. 42

MAURINE LITTLETON GALLERY

Specializes in sculptured glass by modern designers, including American Dale Chihuly.

✚ D3 ✉ 1667 Wisconsin Avenue NW ☎ 202/333–9307 🕐 Tue–Sat 11–6 🚇 Foggy Bottom, then bus No. 32 or 36

MILLENNIUM DECORATIVE ARTS

Furniture, accessories, clothing, and books from 1940 to 1970 along with new products inspired by the styles of the period.

✚ G2 ✉ 1528 U Street NW ☎ 202/483–1218 🕐 Thu–Sun noon–7 🚇 U Street–Cardozo

THE PHOENIX

This is the place to come for Mexican folk crafts, silver jewelry, and natural-fiber native, and contemporary clothing.

✚ D3 ✉ 1514 Wisconsin Avenue NW ☎ 202/338–4404 🕐 Mon–Sat 10–6; Sun 11–5 🚇 Farragut West, then bus No. 35

RETROSPECTIVE

Retrospective sells the things baby-boomers grew up in in the 1940s and 1950s: streamlined designs in metal furniture, clunky tableware, and bold patterns.

✚ F2 ✉ 2324 18th Street NW ☎ 202/483–8112 🕐 Mon, Wed–Fri noon–7; Sat 11–7; Sun noon–6 🚇 Dupont Circle, then bus No. 42

SARAH WESSEL DESIGN

A townhouse full of unusual items including antiques, decorative objects and furnishings.

✚ D3 ✉ 3214 O Street NW ☎ 202/337–1910 🕐 Mon–Sat 11–5:30 🚇 Foggy Bottom, then bus No. 36

SUSQUEHANNA

Susquehanna specializes in American and English furniture and works of art in the largest antique space in Georgetown.

✚ D3 ✉ 3216 O Street NW ☎ 202/333–1511 🕐 Mon–Sat 10–6 🚇 Foggy Bottom, then bus No. 35

SWISS WATCH WORKS

Classic and vintage pocket or wrist watches.

✚ D3 ✉ 1512 Wisconsin Avenue NW ☎ 202/333–4550 🕐 Tue–Fri 10–7; Sat 10–6 🚇 Foggy Bottom, then bus No. 32

Vintage secondhand shopping

The dedicated shopper with an eye for style—but not necessarily at high street prices—can browse in Washington's secondhand shops. Check out Once is not enough for used but stylish men's, women's, and children's clothing and accessories (✚ A2 ✉ 4830 MacArthur Boulevard NW ☎ 202/337–3072 🕐 Mon–Sat 10–5 🚇 Metro Center, then bus No. D6); The Opportunity Shop of the Christ Child Society for vintage clothing, housewares, and antiques (✚ D3 ✉ 1427 Wisconsin Avenue NW ☎ 202/333–6635 🕐 Tue–Sat 10–3:45 🚇 Farragut West, then bus No. 32) and Secondi for women's fashions from Gap to Chanel (✚ F3 ✉ 1702 Connecticut Avenue NW ☎ 202/667–1122 🕐 Mon–Sat 11–6; Sun 1–5 🚇 Dupont Circle).

BOOKS & MUSIC

Books for night owls

You can find bookstores open well into the night in nearly every area of Washington, many with cafés, knowledgeable staff, and discounts. There is always a place to browse. Kramerbooks & Afterwords Café (see main entry this page) is open 24 hours each Saturday and Sunday.

BIRD-IN-HAND BOOKSTORE AND GALLERY

Located in a historic Capital Hill row house, this shop specializes in art, architecture, and design.
✚ K6 ✉ 323 7th Street SE
☎ 202/543–0744 ⏰ Tue–Sat 10–5 🚇 Eastern Market

BORDERS BOOKS AND MUSIC

This spacious outlet of the national chain offers 325,000 titles (including 50,000 music titles) plus a café, readings, signings, and events.
✚ F3 ✉ 18th and L Streets NW
☎ 202/466–4999
⏰ Mon–Thu 8AM–9PM; Fri 8AM–10PM Sat 8AM–9PM
🚇 Farragut West

CHAPTERS LITERARY BOOKSTORE

Specializing in poetry, fiction, and literary criticism, Chapters takes books seriously.
✚ F3 ✉ 1512 K Street NW
☎ 202/347–5495 ⏰ Mon–Fri 10–6:30; Sat 11–5 🚇 McPherson Square

CROWN BOOKS

This national chain specializes in bestsellers, crafts, popular psychology, fiction, and the "kiss'n'tell" books so beloved of Washington scandal-mongers. Everything is heavily discounted.
✚ F3 ✉ 11 Dupont Circle NW
☎ 202/319–1374 ⏰ Daily 9AM–11PM 🚇 Dupont Circle

KEMP MILL MUSIC

This local chain keeps prices low on a full range of CDs and tapes.
✚ F2 ✉ 2459 18th Street NW
☎ 202/387–1011 ⏰ Mon–Fri

8:30AM–9PM; Sat 10–7; Sun noon–5 (both branches) 🚇 Dupont Circle
✚ F4 ✉ 1900 L Street NW
☎ 202/223–5310 🚇 Farragut West

KRAMERBOOKS & AFTERWORDS CAFÉ

The quintessential Washington literary pick-up scene and one of the city's oldest booksellers.
✚ F4 ✉ 1517 Connecticut Avenue NW ☎ 202/387–1400
⏰ Sat, Sun 24 hours; Mon–Thu 7:30AM–1AM 🚇 Dupont Circle

LAMBDA RISING BOOKSTORE

Gay and lesbian books and gifts.
✚ E3 ✉ 1625 Connecticut Avenue NW ☎ 202/462–6969
⏰ Daily 10AM–midnight
🚇 Dupont Circle

LAMMAS WOMEN'S BOOKSTORE & MORE

Books by and for women.
✚ E3 ✉ 1607 17th Street NW
☎ 202/775–8218 ⏰ Mon–Thu, Sat 11–10; Sun 11–8 🚇 Dupont Circle

MELODY RECORD SHOP

Knowledgeable staff and a 10–40 percent discount on CDs, and cassettes.
✚ F3 ✉ 1623 Connecticut Avenue NW ☎ 202/232–4002
⏰ Mon–Thu 10–10; Fri–Sat 10AM–11PM; Sun 11–10
🚇 Farragut North, Dupont Circle

MYSTERYBOOKS

Specializes in puzzle books and the full range of mystery publications.
✚ F3 ✉ 1715 Connecticut Avenue NW ☎ 202/483–1600
⏰ Mon–Fri 11–7; Sat 10–6; Sun noon–5

OLSSON'S BOOKS & RECORDS

The comprehensive stock covers most areas of publishing. Folk and classical recordings come in many formats.

🔲 D3 ✉ 1239 Wisconsin Avenue NW ☎ 202/338–9544
🕐 Mon–Thu 10AM–11PM; Fri–Sat 10AM–midnight; Sun 11–10
Ⓜ Farragut West, then bus No. 32

ORPHEUS RECORDS

All styles of music in most formats. Vinyl hunters come for the good used LPs as well as the best selection of new vinyl in the metropolitan area.

🔲 A5 ✉ 3173 Wilson Boulevard, Arlington, VA ☎ 703/294 6774
🕐 Mon–Sat noon–11; Sun noon–8 Ⓜ Clarendon

POLITICS AND PROSE

The area's largest independent bookstore has comfortable reading chairs, a coffee shop, and knowledgeable staff.

🔲 Off map at E1 ✉ 5015 Connecticut Avenue NW
☎ 202/364–1919 🕐 Sun–Thu 9AM–10:30PM; Fri, Sat 9–9
Ⓜ VanNess, then 15 minutes' walk north

SECOND STORY BOOKS

If used books are your passion, start here. If you don't find your treasure on the acres of shelves, it may be in Second Story's warehouse.

🔲 F3 ✉ 2000 P Street NW ☎ 202/659–8884 🕐 Daily 10–10 Ⓜ Dupont Circle

SISTER'S SPACE & BOOKS

Books by and about African-American women are the focus here.

🔲 G2 ✉ 1515 U Street NW ☎ 202/332–3433 🕐 Mon–Sat 10–7; Sun noon–5
Ⓜ U Street–Cardozo

TOWER RECORDS

Loud and hip, Tower has the largest selection of cassettes and CDs in Washington.

🔲 E4 ✉ 2000 Pennsylvania Avenue NW ☎ 202/331–2400
🕐 Daily 9AM–midnight Ⓜ Foggy Bottom

TRAVEL BOOKS & LANGUAGE

TB&L has been called the Library of Congress of travel book stores, stocking the nation's largest selection of maps, classic and historical travel literature, architectural and relocation guides. You'll find 140 languages and dialects represented and many cultural events are on offer.

🔲 Off map at C1 ✉ 4437 Wisconsin Avenue NW ☎ 202/237–1322; 800/220–2665
🕐 Mon–Sat 10–10; Sun noon–7 Ⓜ America U/Tenley Town

U.S. GOVERNMENT BOOKSTORE

On hand here are the countless publications produced by the Feds, including research reports on a huge range of subjects.

🔲 G4 ✉ 1510 H Street NW ☎ 202/653–5075 🕐 Mon–Fri 8:30–4:30 Ⓜ McPherson Square

VERTIGO BOOKS

Specializes in African-American as well as international writers.

🔲 F3 ✉ 1337 Connecticut Avenue, NW ☎ 202/429–9272
🕐 Mon–Fri 10–7; Sat 11–7; Sun noon–5 Ⓜ Dupont Circle

Special-interest tomes

Specialty books can be located at the headquarters of the the hundreds of professional associations, think tanks, and foundations that make Washington home—the Brookings Institution, the Carnegie Endowment for International Peace, the Freedom Forum, the American Association of Museums, the American Institute of Architects, and even the American Society of Association Executives. If you've got an interest in architecture, bee-keeping, chemistry, or zoology, you can find both popular and scholarly editions for your passion.

LIVE MUSIC & COMEDY CLUBS

Night options

Washington clubs offer every kind of music. You can have it live or played by a DJ. You can dance or just listen. Or check out one of the murder mystery dinners, whodunits where the audience gets involved with the story while watching it. The Blair Mansion Inn (✉ 7711 Eastern Avenue, Silver Spring, MD ☎ 301/588–6646) and Murder Upon Request (✉ Old Arlington Hilton Hotel, 950 N Stafford Street, Arlington ☎ 703/379–8108) have weekend shows.

LIVE MUSIC

9:30 CLUB

This trendy club is hot in summer, cold in winter and always dark and smoky, but you can't beat it for local, national, and international progressive music.
✚ G4 ✉ 815 V Street NW ☎ 202/393–0930 🕐 Generally Sun–Thu 7:30PM–midnight; Fri, Sat 9PM–2AM 🚇 Metro Center 💲 Cover charge. Tickets at the door or from TicketMaster

BIRCHMERE

The best place in the area to hear national acoustic folk and bluegrass acts, plus occasional rockabilly or rock.
✚ Off map at E10 ✉ 3701 Mount Vernon Avenue, Alexandria, VA ☎ 703/549–7500 🕐 Sun–Thu 6:30PM–11PM; Fri, Sat 7PM–12:30AM

BLUES ALLEY

Washington's best jazz club serves up national jazz acts, such as Ramsey Lewis and Charlie Byrd. The Creole cooking is not bad, either.
✚ D3 ✉ Rear 1073 Wisconsin Avenue NW ☎ 202/337–4141 🕐 Sun–Thu 6PM–midnight; Fri, Sat 6PM–2AM. Shows at 8 and 10, plus occasional midnight shows Fri and Sat 🚇 Farragut West, then bus No. 32 or 38B 💲 Cover charge and minimum charge

THE GARAGE

This club hosts a wide variety of bands, from alternative and traditional rock to blues, reggae, and hip-hop.
✚ F3 ✉ 1214 18th Street NW ☎ 202/331–7123 🕐 Open when there is a show, usually until 1AM 🚇 Dupont Circle

METRO CAFE

Usually features newer, alternative-type rock acts; also occasional films and theater performances.
✚ G3 ✉ 1522 14th Street NW ✉ 202/518–7900 🕐 Mon–Thu 7PM–2AM; Fri, Sat 7PM–3AM; Sun 7PM–2AM 🚇 Dupont Circle

MURPHY'S

With a name like Murphy's, you know it's going to be Irish music. Live music isn't nightly, so call ahead.
✚ E4 ✉ 2609 24th Street NW ☎ 202/462–7171 🕐 Sun–Thu 11AM–1:30AM; Fri, Sat 11AM–2:30AM 🚇 Foggy Bottom

ONE STEP DOWN

Smoky, low-ceilinged, and intimate like all good jazz clubs. It also has the best jazz jukebox in town. Local acts and New York jazz artists live Wednesday to Saturday.
✚ E4 ✉ 2517 Pennsylvania Avenue NW ☎ 202/955–7141 🕐 Mon–Thu 10AM–2AM; Fri 10AM–3AM; Sat noon–3AM; Sun noon–2AM 🚇 Foggy Bottom 💲 Cover charge and minimum charge

COMEDY

CAPITOL STEPS

Political musical revues weekends at various venues.
☎ 703/683–8330

GROSS NATIONAL PRODUCT

Political satire on Saturdays at Chief Ike's.
✚ F1 ✉ 1725 Columbia Road NW ☎ 202/783–7212 🕐 Mon–Thu 4PM–2AM; Fri 4PM–3AM; Sat noon–3AM; Sun 4PM–2AM 🚇 Dupont Circle, then bus No. 42

Bars & Lounges

BRICKSKELLER
With more than 800 brands of beer, from Central American lagers to U.S. microbrews, this is Washington's premier pub. Bartenders oblige beer-can collectors by opening the containers from the bottom.
✚ E3 ✉ 1523 22nd Street NW ☎ 202/293–1885 🕐 Mon–Thu 11:30AM–2AM; Fri 11:30AM–3AM; Sat 6AM–3AM; Sun 6PM–2AM 🚇 Dupont Circle

CAPITOL CITY BREWING COMPANY
This microbrewery, the first brewery in Washington since Prohibition, makes everything from a bitter to a bock, though not all types are available at all times. At the gleaming copper bar, metal steps lead up to the brewing tanks.
✚ G4 ✉ 1100 New York Avenue NW ☎ 202/628–2222 🕐 Mon–Sat 11AM–2AM; Sun 11AM–midnight 🚇 Metro Center

CHAMPIONS
In one of D.C.'s biggest sports bars, the walls are covered with jerseys, pucks, bats, and balls, and the big game of the evening is always showing on the big screen.
✚ D3 ✉ 1206 Wisconsin Avenue NW ☎ 202/965–4005 🕐 Mon–Thu 5AM–2AM; Fri 5PM–3AM; Sat 11:30AM–3AM; Sun 11:30AM–2AM. One-drink minimum Fri and Sat after 10PM 🚇 Farragut West, then bus No. 32

THE DUBLINER
The closest thing in Washington to an Irish pub, this is a favorite with Capitol Hill staffers.
✚ J4 ✉ 4 F Street NW ☎ 202/737–3773 🕐 Sun–Thu 11AM–1:30AM; Fri, Sat 11AM–2:30AM 🚇 Union Station

HAWK'N'DOVE
A friendly neighborhood bar, frequented by political types, lobbyists, and Marines (from a nearby barracks).
✚ J6 ✉ 329 Pennsylvania Avenue SE ☎ 202/543–3300 🕐 Sun–Thu 10AM–2AM; Fri, Sat 10AM–3AM 🚇 Capitol South

OZIO
One of Washington's first cigar-and-martini bars, Ozio still attracts K Street lawyers and lobbyists.
✚ F4 ✉ 1835 K Street NW ☎ 202/822–6000 🕐 Sun–Thu noon–2AM; Fri, Sat noon–3AM 🚇 Farragut North or Farragut West

SIGN OF THE WHALE
Well-known post-Preppie/neo-Yuppie haven right in the heart of a densely bar-populated area downtown.
✚ F3 ✉ 1825 M Street NW ☎ 202/785–1110 🕐 Sun–Thu 11:30AM–2AM; Fri, Sat 11:30AM–3AM 🚇 Farragut North

YACHT CLUB
Just across the city limits in Maryland, this lounge is popular with well-dressed, middle-aged singles. Jacket and tie or turtleneck required (casual Wednesday).
✚ Off map at C1 ✉ 8111 Woodmont Avenue, Bethesda, MD ☎ 301/654–2396 🕐 Tue–Thu 5PM–1AM; Fri 5PM–2AM; Sat 8AM–2AM.

Where the action is

Washington has pockets of activity downtown and in its more ethnically diverse neighborhoods. Adams-Morgan, around 18th Street and Columbia Road, has many bars, clubs, and restaurants. Capitol Hill (especially along Pennsylvania Avenue SE), the U Street NW corridor (from about 14th Street to 18th Street), and the downtown area (around 19th and M Streets NW), are also fairly dense with nighttime activities.

THEATERS

Tickets

Buy tickets in person at the Old Post Office Pavilion (✉ 1100 Pennsylvania Avenue NW ◷ Tue–Sat 11–6). Tickets for Sunday and Monday performances are sold on Saturday. There is a 10 percent service charge per order.

Tickets to most events are sold by three main ticket outlets as well as by the box office.

TicketMaster (☎ 202/432–7328) sells tickets by phone and at some stores, including Hecht and Company, to concerts, sports events, and many special events.

Protix (☎ 703/218–6500) has tickets to shows at Wolf Trap and some other venues.

TicketPlace (☎ 202/842–5387) sells half-price, day-of-performance tickets for selected shows (it is also a full-price TicketMaster outlet).

ARENA STAGE
Arena manages a long season in its three theaters: the theater-in-the-round Arena, the proscenium Kreeger, and the cabaret-style Old Vat Room. The New Voices series offers the chance to see new plays in development at reduced prices.
✚ H7 ✉ 6th Street and Maine Avenue SW ☎ 202/488–3300 Ⓜ Waterfront

FORD'S THEATER
The theater where President Abraham Lincoln was assassinated now mostly mounts musicals (Dickens's *A Christmas Carol* is presented every December).
✚ G4 ✉ 511 10th Street NW ☎ 202/347–4833 Ⓜ Metro Center

GALA HISPANIC THEATER
Spanish classics as well as contemporary and modern Latin-American plays in both Spanish and English.
✚ Off map at F1 ✉ 1625 Park Road NW ☎ 202/234–7174 Dupont Circle, then bus No. 42

NATIONAL THEATER
Destroyed by fire and rebuilt four times, the National Theater has operated in the same location since 1835. It presents pre- and post-Broadway shows.
✚ G4 ✉ 1321 Pennsylvania Avenue NW ☎ 202/628–6161 Ⓜ Metro Center

SHAKESPEARE THEATER
The season here includes five plays, three by the Bard and two by other playwrights.
✚ H5 ✉ 450 7th Street NW ☎ 202/547–1122 Ⓜ Archives–Navy Memorial

SIGNATURE THEATER
Its five-play season ranges from contemporary renditions of classics and musicals to new drama.
✚ B10 ✉ 3806 South Four Mile Run Drive, Arlington, VA ☎ 703/218–6500 Ⓜ Pentagon, then bus No. 22A, 22B or 22C

SOURCE THEATER
The 107-seat Source Theater presents established plays and modern interpretations of classics. Each July and August, Source hosts a series of new plays, many by local playwrights.
✚ G2 ✉ 1835 14th Street NW ☎ 202/462–1073 Ⓜ U Street–Cardozo

STUDIO THEATER
One of Washington's nicest independent company theaters, Studio performs classics and offbeat plays. The 50-seat Secondstage mounts experimental works.
✚ G3 ✉ 1333 P Street NW ☎ 202/332–3300 Ⓜ Dupont Circle

WARNER THEATER
Theater and dance performances, as well as some pop music shows.
✚ G4 ✉ 13th and E Streets NW ☎ 202/783–4000 Ⓜ Metro Center

WOOLLY MAMMOTH THEATER COMPANY
Experimental and contemporary plays.
✚ G3 ✉ 1401 Church Street NW ☎ 202/393–3939 Ⓜ Dupont Circle

CONCERT VENUES

D.A.R. CONSTITUTION HALL
Formerly home of the National Symphony Orchestra, this 3,700-seat hall hosts musical performances, staged shows, and occasional big-name comedy acts.
➕ F5 ✉ 18th and D Streets NW ☎ 202/638–2661 🚇 Farragut West, then walk six blocks south)

GEORGE MASON UNIVERSITY
The GMU campus in suburban Virginia is home to the Center for the Arts. The Patriot Center, also on campus, holds concerts and sporting events.
➕ Off map at A2 ✉ Route 123 and Braddock Road, Fairfax, VA ☎ Center for the Arts 703/993–8888; Patriot Center 703/993–3000 or 202/432–7328

LISNER AUDITORIUM
This 1,500-seat theater, on the George Washington University campus, presents pop, classical, and choral concerts.
➕ F4 ✉ 21st and H Streets NW ☎ 202/994–1500 🚇 Foggy Bottom

MERRIWEATHER POST PAVILION
An hour north of the District, this outdoor pavilion with covered seating hosts big-name acts in summer.
➕ Off map at M1 ✉ 10475 Little Patuxent Parkway, Columbia, MD ☎ 301/982–1800; tickets 703/218–6500

NATIONAL GALLERY OF ART
The National Gallery Orchestra, as well as outside recitalists and ensembles, hold free

concerts in the West Building's West Garden Court on Sunday evenings from October to June.
➕ H5 ✉ 6th Street and Constitution Avenue NW ☎ 202/842–6941 🚇 Archives–Navy Memorial

NISSAN PAVILION AT STONE RIDGE
This 25,000-seat venue near Manassas hosts rock, country and pop concerts.
➕ Off map at A5 ✉ 7800 Cellar Door Drive, Gainesville, VA ☎ 703/754–6400 or 202/432–7328

SMITHSONIAN INSTITUTION
An assortment of music—both free and ticketed—at various locations. The Smithsonian Associates Program (☎ 202/357–3030) offers everything from a cappella groups to Cajun zydeco bands.
➕ G5, H5, H4 ✉ At various Smithsonian museums, most of which are on the Mall ☎ 202/357–2700 🚇 Smithsonian

MCI CENTER
The 20,000-seat home of Washington's pro basketball and hockey teams also has regular pop concerts.
➕ H4 ✉ 601 F Street NW, ☎ Information 202/628–3200; tickets 202/432–7328 🚇 Gallery Place, Chinatown

WOLF TRAP FARM PARK
About 20 minutes' drive from Washington, you can picnic in the national park before taking in an opera, dance or concert.
➕ Off map at A2 ✉ 1624 Trap Road, Vienna VA ☎ Information 703/255–1900; tickets 703/255–1860

John F. Kennedy Center for the Performing Arts
The John F. Kennedy Center (➤ 25) is indeed a center for cultural events, with five separate stages under one roof: the Concert Hall, home to the National Symphony Orchestra; the Opera House, for ballet, modern dance, opera, and large-scale musicals; the Eisenhower Theater, usually used for drama; the Terrace Theater, a smaller stage for chamber groups and experimental works; and the Theater Lab.
➕ E4 ✉ New Hampshire Avenue and Rock Creek Parkway ☎ 202/467–4600 or 800/444–1324 🚇 Foggy Bottom

American folklife
The Smithsonian's Festival of American Folklife provides an alternative to high culture and fine art. Each year the Smithsonian celebrates one country, one state, one profession, and a number of musical folk traditions. Summer temperatures persuade bureaucrats and others to join in early evening, open-air dance parties.

THE PERFORMING ARTS & MOVIES

Movies

Check the daily newspapers for mainstream first-run movies; theaters are scattered throughout the city. For less mainstream first-run and foreign films, try the Cineplex Odeon theaters such as Dupont Circle, Inner Circle of Janus 3 (☎ 202/333–FILM, which translates to 3456). For revivals and foreign, independent, and avant-garde films, try the American Film Institute (✉ Kennedy Center ☎ 202/785–4600). The Hirshhorn Museum (☎ 202/357–2700), National Gallery of Art East Building (☎ 202/737–4215), and National Archives (☎ 202/501–5000), all on the Mall, often show historical, unusual, or experimental films. The Library of Congress (☎ 202/707–5677) often shows old movies, including some silent films. Filmfest D.C. (☎ 202/274–6810), an annual citywide festival of international cinema, takes place in late April and early May.

CHAMBER MUSIC

CORCORAN GALLERY OF ART
✚ F4–F5 ✉ 17th Street and New York Avenue NW ☎ 202/639–1700 🕐 Periodically throughout the year

FOLGER SHAKESPEARE LIBRARY
The Folger Consort plays medieval, Renaissance, and baroque music.
✚ J5 ✉ 201 East Capitol Street SE ☎ 202/544–7077 🕐 Oct–May

NATIONAL ACADEMY OF SCIENCES
✚ E5 ✉ 2101 Constitution Avenue NW ☎ 202/334–2436 🕐 Oct–May 🆓 Free

PHILLIPS COLLECTION
✚ F3 ✉ 1600 21st Street NW ☎ 202/387–2151 🕐 Sep–May: Sun 5PM

CONCERT SERIES

ARMED FORCES CONCERT SERIES
The Capitol's East Terrace and the Sylvan Theater near the Washington Monument.
☎ Air Force 202/767–5658; Army 703/696–3399; Navy 202/433–2525; Marines 202/433–4011 🕐 Jun–Aug: Mon–Fri evenings

CARTER BARRON AMPHITHEATER
Pop, jazz, and gospel music. The Shakespeare Theater (► 80) presents a free play outdoors in June.
✚ Off map at F1 ✉ 16th Street and Colorado Avenue NW ☎ 202/426–0486 🕐 Mid-Jun–Aug: Sat, Sun

CHORAL GROUPS

CHORAL ARTS SOCIETY
A 180-voice choir performs at the Kennedy Center (► 25).
🕐 Periodically throughout the year, plus three Christmas sing-alongs

WASHINGTON NATIONAL CATHEDRAL
Choral and church groups (► 59).

SHRINE OF THE IMMACULATE CONCEPTION
Venue for choral groups (► 47).

DANCE

DANCE PLACE
Modern and ethnic dance.
✚ Off map at K1 ✉ 3225 8th Street NE ☎ 202/269–1600 🕐 Sat, Sun

JOY OF MOTION
Home to area troupes.
✚ Off map at C1 ✉ 1643 Connecticut Avenue NW ☎ 202/387–0911

MOUNT VERNON COLLEGE
Hosts visiting dance companies, fall and spring.
✚ B2 ✉ 2100 Foxhall Road NW ☎ 202/625–4655

THE SMITHSONIAN ASSOCIATES PROGRAM
Dance groups perform at Smithsonian museums.
☎ 202/357–3030

THE WASHINGTON BALLET
Ballet performances, plus *The Nutcracker* in December
☎ 202/362–3606

SPORTS

BIKING

Some of the best rides are along the George Washington Memorial Parkway, along the Virginia side of the Potomac River to Mount Vernon (35 miles round trip); the C & O Canal towpath from Georgetown to Cumberland, MD (180 miles one way); and through Rock Creek Park.

WASHINGTON AREA BICYCLIST ASSOCIATION
Information on bike trails in and around Washington.
✉ 818 Connecticut Avenue NW, Suite 300, 20006
☎ 202/628–2500

Rent bicycles from:
BICYCLE PRO SHOP
✉ 3403 M Street NW Boulevard, Alexandria, VA
☎ 202/337–0311

BIG WHEEL BIKES
✉ 1034 33rd Street NW, Georgetown ☎ 202/337–0254

CITY BIKES
✉ 2501 Champlain Street NW
☎ 202/265–1564

DISTRICT HARDWARE
✉ 2003 P Street NW
☎ 202/659–8686

METROPOLIS BICYCLES
Also rents rollerblades.
✉ 709 8th Street SE, Capitol Hill
☎ 202/543–8900

BOATING

FLETCHER'S BOAT HOUSE
Rowboats, canoes, and bicycles for rent.
✉ C & O Canal towpath, 2 miles north of Georgetown, near Reservoir Road NW
☎ 202/244–0461

THOMPSON'S BOAT CENTER
Rents canoes, rowboats, rowing shells, sailboards, and bicycles.
✉ Virginia Avenue and Rock Creek Park, behind Kennedy Center ☎ 202/333–4861

Paddle boats are available in summer on the east side of the Tidal Basin in front of the Jefferson Memorial.
☎ 202/479–2426

GOLF

Washington has three public golf courses:
HAINS POINT
✉ East Potomac Park near the Jefferson Memorial
☎ 202/554–7660

LANGSTON GOLF COURSE
✉ 26th Street and Benning Road NE ☎ 202/397–8638

ROCK CREEK PARK
✉ 16th and Rittenhouse Streets NW ☎ 202/882–7332

In the suburbs:
RESTON NATIONAL
✉ 11875 Sunrise Valley Drive, Reston, VA ☎ 703/620–9333

NORTHWEST PARK
✉ 15701 Layhill Road, Wheaton, MD ☎ 301/598–6100

TENNIS

The District of Columbia has 144 outdoor courts.
✉ Department of Recreation, 3149 16th Street NW, 20010
☎ 202/673–7646

Spectator sports

If you are here in fall, you will hear about the Redskins football team, but season-ticket holders have all the seats. You'll have better luck seeing the Wizards play basketball or the Capitals play hockey, both at the MCI Center in downtown Washington. For tickets, call TicketMaster
☎ 202/ 432–7328.

83

LUXURY HOTELS

Hotel Prices

Expect to pay the following prices per night for a double room (excluding 13 percent tax—9.75 percent in Virginia—plus $1.50 per night occupancy tax). When you make your reservation it's always worth asking whether any special deals are available.

Budget   up to $150
Mid-range   up to $250
Luxury   more than $250

Booking agencies

Capitol Reservations
Books rooms at over 70 hotels at 20–40 percent off rack rates ☎ 202/452–1270 or 800/847–4832 🕐 Mon–Fri 8:30–6:30

Washington D.C. Accommodations
Books rooms in any hotel in town, with discounts of 20–40 percent available at about 40 locations ☎ 202/289–2220 or 800/ 554–2220 🕐 Mon–Fri 9–6

FOUR SEASONS HOTEL

On the eastern edge of Georgetown, this hotel is known as a gathering place for Washington's elite.
✚ E3 ✉ 2800 Pennsylvania Avenue NW ☎ 202/342–0444 or 800/332–3442, fax 202/944–2076 🚇 Foggy Bottom

HAY-ADAMS HOTEL

Looking like a mansion on the outside and an English country house within, this hotel has a picture-postcard White House view—ask for a room on the south side.
✚ F4 ✉ 800 16th Street NW ☎ 202/638–6600 or 800/424–5054, fax 202/638–2716 🚇 McPherson Square

JEFFERSON HOTEL

Small luxury hotel with outstanding service done up in federal-style.
✚ F3 ✉ 1200 16th Street NW ☎ 202/347–2200 or 800/368–5966, fax 202/223–9039 🚇 Farragut North

PARK HYATT

A notable collection of modern art adorns this hotel. Reproductions of Chinese antiques accent the rooms, a mix of traditional and contemporary styles.
✚ E3 ✉ 1201 24th Street NW ☎ 202/ 789–1234 or 800/233–1234, fax 202/457– 8823 🚇 Foggy Bottom

RITZ-CARLTON, PENTAGON CITY

Public spaces in this hotel display a $2 million art and antiques collection. Many guest rooms have a view of the monuments across the Potomac.
✚ D8 ✉ 1250 S Hayes Street Arlington, VA ☎ 703/415–5000 or 800/241–3333, fax 703/415–5061 🚇 Pentagon City

STOUFFER RENAISSANCE MAYFLOWER

The ornate lobby glistens with gilded trim and the rooms feature custom-designed furniture.
✚ F4 ✉ 1127 Connecticut Avenue NW ☎ 202/347–3000 or 800/468–3571, fax 202/766–9184 🚇 Farragut North

SWISSOTEL WASHINGTON, THE WATERGATE

Best known for its part in the fall of Richard Nixon, this hotel has large rooms, most with river views and many with balconies.
✚ E4 ✉ 2650 Virginia Avenue NW ☎ 202/965–2300 or 800/424–2736, fax 202/337–7915 🚇 Foggy Bottom

WESTIN FAIRFAX

Lovely hotel with European furnishings and 18th- and 19th-century English art.
✚ F3 ✉ 2100 Massachusetts Avenue NW ☎ 202/293–2100 or 800/241–3333, fax 202/835–2196 🚇 Dupont Circle

WILLARD INTER-CONTINENTAL

Heads of state have made the Willard, steps from the White House, home since 1853. The lobby is *beaux-arts*, the rooms quite plain.
✚ G4 ✉ 1401 Pennsylvania Avenue NW ☎ 202/628–9100 or 800/327–0200, fax 202/637–7326 🚇 McPherson Square

MID-RANGE HOTELS

CAPITOL HILL SUITES
This all-suite hotel is tucked away behind the Madison Building of the Library of Congress.
✚ J6 ✉ 200 C Street SE
☎ 202/543–6000 or 800/424–9165, fax 202/547–2608
Ⓜ Capitol South

DOUBLETREE GUEST SUITES
These all-suite hotels are close to Georgetown and the Kennedy Center.
✚ E4 ✉ 801 New Hampshire Avenue NW ☎ 202/785–2000 or 800/424–2900, fax 202/785–9485) Ⓜ Foggy Bottom
✚ E4 ✉ 2500 Pennsylvania Avenue NW ☎ 202/333–8060 or 800/424–2900, fax 202/338–3818 Ⓜ Foggy Bottom

HENLEY PARK HOTEL
A bit of Britain in a developing neighborhood, this is a National Trust for Historic Preservation designated Historic Hotel.
✚ G4 ✉ 926 Massachusetts Avenue NW ☎ 202/638–5200 or 800/222–8474, fax 202/414–0513 Ⓜ Metro Center/Gallery Place

HOTEL WASHINGTON
Well-known for its view, this lovely hotel is just a block from the White House, which you can see from the rooftop Sky Terrace from May through October.
✚ G4 ✉ 515 15th Street NW
☎ 202/638–5900 or 800/424–9540, fax 202/638–1594
Ⓜ Metro Center

HOTEL MONTICELLO
This homey, all-suite hotel is on a side street in Georgetown.
✚ D4 ✉ 1075 Thomas Jefferson Street NW ☎ 202/337–0900 or 800/333–0124, fax 202/333–6526

LATHAM HOTEL
This small, colonial-style hotel on one of Georgetown's main streets offers views of busy M Street or the C & O Canal. Its Citronelle restaurant is one of Washington's best.
✚ D3 ✉ 3000 M Street NW
☎ 202/726–5000 or 800/368–5922, fax 202/337–4250

MORRISON-CLARK INN HOTEL
Created by merging two 1864 townhouses, this inn is another of the National Trust for Historic Preservation designated Historic Hotels. The restaurant is well regarded.
✚ G4 ✉ 1015 L Street NW
☎ 202/898–1200 or 800/332–7898, fax 202/289–8576
Ⓜ Mt. Vernon Square–UDC

NORMANDY INN
This European-style hotel is on a quiet street in the exclusive Connecticut Avenue embassy area. There is a wine and cheese reception every Tuesday evening.
✚ E2 ✉ 2118 Wyoming Avenue NW ☎ 202/483–1350 or 800/424–3729, fax 202/387–8241

RIVER INN
This small, all-suite hotel is near Georgetown, George Washington University, and the Kennedy Center. Rooms are homey if modest.
✚ E4 ✉ 924 25th Street NW
☎ 202/337–7600 or 800/424–2741, fax 202/337–6520
Ⓜ Foggy Bottom

Washington hotels
Most major chains have hotels in the city and the nearby suburbs. For a complete list of hotels, contact the Washington, D.C., Convention and Visitors Association (✉ 1212 New York Avenue NW, Washington, D.C., 20005 ☎ 202/789–7000). All the hotels here are air-conditioned. Nearly all the finer hotels have superb restaurants whose traditionally high prices are almost always completely justified.

BUDGET ACCOMMODATIONS

Bed & breakfast

To find reasonably priced accommodations in small guest houses and private homes, contact either of the following bed-and-breakfast services: Bed 'n' Breakfast Accommodations Ltd. of Washington, D.C., (✉ Box 12011, Washington, D.C., 20005 ☎ 202/328–3510); or Bed and Breakfast League Ltd. (✉ Box 9490, Washington, D.C., 20016–9490 ☎ 202/363–7767). If you must have a private bath, make it clear when you book.

BEST WESTERN DOWNTOWN CAPITOL HILL

Furnished in typical chain budget-hotel fashion, this is located near several tourist sites, including the National Building Museum, Union Station, the MCI Center, and Chinatown.
✚ H4 ✉ 724 Third Street NW ☎ 202/842–4466 or 800/242–4831, fax 202/842–4831 Ⓜ Judiciary Square

DAYS INN CONNECTICUT AVENUE

Standard hotel away from downtown, but only two blocks from the Metro.
✚ Off map at E1 ✉ 4400 Connecticut Avenue NW ☎ 202/244–5600 or 800/325–2525, fax 202/244–6794 Ⓜ Van Ness

HOLIDAY INN EISENHOWER

A bargain for the budget traveler, near Old Town in Alexandria.
✚ Off map at E10 ✉ 2460 Eisenhower Avenue, Alexandria, VA ☎ 703/960–3400 or 800/465–4329, fax 703/329–0953 Ⓜ Eisenhower

HOTEL HARRINGTON

This is your basic clean, no-frills hotel, but with a great location. The Mall and many museums are just a few blocks away.
✚ G4 ✉ 436 11th Street NW ☎ 202/628–8140 or 800/424–8532, fax 202/347–3924 Ⓜ Metro Center

HOTEL TABARD INN

Three Victorian townhouses joined together. Charmingly well-worn furnishings.
✚ F3 ✉ 1739 N Street NW ☎ 202/785–1277, fax 202/785–6173 Ⓜ Dupont Circle

HOWARD JOHNSON'S EXPRESS INN

On one of the main routes into the city.
✚ K3 ✉ 600 New York Avenue NE ☎ 202/546–9200 or 800/446–4656, fax 202/546–6348 Ⓜ Rhode Island, then bus No. P6

KALORAMA GUEST HOUSE

Five separate early 20th-century townhouses, decorated with old-fashioned charm. There are no phones or T.V.s (except in suites), but breakfast and afternoon aperitifs are included.
✚ F2 ✉ 1854 Mintwood Place NW ☎ 202/667–6369, fax 202/319–1262 Ⓜ Woodley Park–Zoo
✚ E1 ✉ 2700 Cathedral Avenue NW ☎ 202/328–0860, fax 202/328–8730 Ⓜ Woodley Park–Zoo

WASHINGTON INTERNATIONAL AYH-HOSTEL

Well-kept hostel with bunk-bedded dormitory rooms; families may get their own rooms if the hostel is not full.
✚ G4 ✉ 1009 11th Street NW ☎ 202/737–2333, fax 202/737–1508 Ⓜ McPherson Square

WINDSOR PARK HOTEL

Rooms in this small hotel are decorated in Queen Anne-style with period art, and each has a small refrigerator. Free Continental breakfast.
✚ E2 ✉ 2116 Kalorama Road NW ☎ 202/483–7700 or 800/247–3064, fax 202/332–4547 Woodley Park–Zoo

WASHINGTON
travel facts

ARRIVING & DEPARTING

Planning your trip

- In spring, the most crowded season, the city is alive with flowers and blossoming trees, including the must-see-to-believe cherry blossoms around the Tidal Basin and Washington Monument. Fall is attractive too, especially mid-October when the leaves are changing color, and the milder weather often extends into December The city is less busy during fall and winter. The heat can take its toll in the summer, but there are always lots of free activities, including nightly military band concerts, the Smithsonian's Folklife Festival on the Mall in July, and noontime and evening concerts around town.

Climate

- Spring and fall are lovely in Washington, with average high temperatures of between 59°F and 77°F.
- Summers are very hot and humid, with temperatures sometimes reaching 95°F or more.
- Winters can be variable: a year of record cold weather and below-freezing temperatures can be followed by one of the warmest winters ever.
- Snowfall is unpredictable, and always shuts the city down.

Arriving by air

- The major gateways to Washington, D.C., include: Ronald Reagan National Airport ☎ 703/417–8000 in Virginia, four miles south of downtown Washington; Dulles International Airport ☎ 703/572–2700 26 miles west of Washington; Baltimore-Washington International (BWI) Airport ☎ 410/859–7100 in Maryland, about 25 miles northeast of Washington.
- Flying time is one hour from New York, two hours from Chicago, and five hours, 40 minutes from Los Angeles.
- Major air carriers serving the three airports include:
  Air Canada ☎ 800/776–3000
  Air France ☎ 800/237–2747
  All Nippon Airways ☎ 800/235–9262
  America West ☎ 800/235–9292
  American Airlines ☎ 800/433–7300
  British Airways ☎ 800/247–9297
  Continental ☎ 800/525–0280
  Delta ☎ 800/221–1212
  El Al ☎ 800/223–6700
  Icelandair ☎ 800/223–5500
  Japan Air Lines ☎ 800/525–3663
  KLM Royal Dutch ☎ 800/374–7747
  Lufthansa ☎ 800/645–3880
  Midwest Express ☎ 800/452–2022
  Northwest ☎ 800/225–2525
  Saudi Arabian Airlines ☎ 800/472–8342
  Swissair ☎ 800/221–4750
  TWA ☎ 800/221–2000
  United ☎ 800/241–6522
  US Airways ☎ 800/428–4322
- For inexpensive, no-frills flights, contact Southwest Airlines ☎ 800/435–9792
- To register complaints about charter and scheduled airlines, contact the U.S. Department of Transportation's Aviation Consumer Protection Division, C-75, Room 4107, Washington, D.C., 20590 ☎ 202/366–2220 or, for safety issues, call the hotline ☎ 800/322–7873.

Taxi to downtown

- The fare for one person to downtown from Reagan National is about $15 (plus a $1.25 surcharge); from Dulles, $45; and from BWI, $55–$60.

• Bus to downtown

The Washington Flyer ☎ 703/685–1400 goes from Dulles airport to the Convention Center at New York Avenue and 11th Street NW. Buses leave the airport every half hour. The 45-minute trip costs $16 ($26 round-trip). Inter-airport service is available between Dulles and Reagan National airports for the same price ($16 one-way, $26 round-trip). Cash, Visa and MasterCard are accepted.

• SuperShuttle ☎ 800/809–7080 offers airport-to-door service from all three airports. Fares to downtown locations are approximately $9 per person from Reagan National, $20 (plus $10 each additional person) from Dulles, and $28 (plus $5 each additional person) from BWI.

Train to downtown

• Free shuttle buses run between airline terminals and the train station at BWI airport.

• Amtrak ☎ 800/872–7245 and MARC (Maryland Rail Commuter Service) ☎ 800/325–7245 trains run between BWI and Union Station from around 6AM to midnight.

• The cost of the 40-minute ride is $17 on Amtrak, $5 on MARC (Monday–Friday only).

Metro to downtown

• The blue and yellow Metro lines run from Reagan National to downtown, with stations next to Terminals B and C. Fare cards can be bought from machines on level 2 near the pedestrian bridges linking the two terminals. For Metro information ☎ 202/637–7000 ◉ Mon–Thu 5:30AM–midnight; Fri, Sat 8AM–1AM; Sun 8AM–midnight.

Limousine to downtown

• Private Car ☎ 800/685–0888 has two counters at BWI airport ($63 to downtown for up to four passengers in a luxury sedan; $68 for a six-passenger limousine), or call ahead for a car to meet you at either Reagan National ($45 for a sedan, $55 for a limousine) or Dulles ($73 for a sedan, $81 for a limousine). Fares are approximate, and there is an additional 15 percent gratuity.

ESSENTIAL FACTS

Money matters

• Sales tax in Washington, D.C., is 5.75 percent on top of the marked goods price.

• Hotel tax is 13 percent (9.75 percent in Virginia) extra on the room rate, with $1.50 occupancy tax per night.

• Restaurant tax is 10 percent.

Etiquette

• Smoking is less and less welcome in Washington. It has been banned from the workplace (people huddle at the entrances of office buildings for their smoke breaks), and public buildings such as museums and theaters generally do not allow smoking anywhere. One exception is Georgetown Mall, where smoking is permitted in the common areas but not in the stores. While most restaurants have separate smoking and nonsmoking sections, some ban it outright. If you don't see an ashtray, don't light up without asking. Bars remain the last bastion of smokers' rights—so be aware that when you leave one you smell like an ashtray.

Places of worship
- Episcopal: Washington National Cathedral ✉ Wisconsin and Massachusetts Avenues NW ☎ 202/537–6200
- Jewish: Adas Israel ✉ Connecticut Avenue and Porter Street NW ☎ 202/362–4433
- Muslim: Islamic Mosque and Cultural Center ✉ 2551 Massachusetts Avenue NW ☎ 202/332–8343
- Roman Catholic: National Shrine of the Immaculate Conception ✉ Michigan Avenue and 4th Street NE ☎ 202/526–8300; Franciscan Monastery ✉ 14th and Quincy Streets NE ☎ 202/526–6800

Time
- Washington, D.C., is on Eastern Standard Time, three hours ahead of Pacific Standard Time, two hours ahead of Mountain Standard Time, and one hour ahead of Central Standard Time. For Daylight Saving Time clocks are moved forward one hour on the first Sunday of April, and go back one hour on the last Sunday in October.
- For the current time ☎ 202/844–2525.

Visitor Information
- Washington, D.C., Convention and Visitors Association ✉ 1212 New York Avenue NW, 6th Floor, Washington, D.C., 20005 ☎ 202/789–7000, fax 202/789–7037; also ✉ 1300 Pennsylvania Avenue NW 🕐 Enquiries on Sat and Sun
- D.C. Committee to Promote Washington ✉ 1212 New York Avenue NW, 2nd Floor, Washington, D.C., 20005 ☎ 800/422–8644
- National Park Service ✉ Office of Public Affairs, National Capital Region, 1100 Ohio Drive SW, Washington, D.C., 20242 ☎ 202/619–7222
- The White House Visitor Center ✉ Baldridge Hall in the Department of Commerce Building, 1450 Pennsylvania Avenue NW ☎ 202/208–1631 has information on White House tours and special events.
- National Park Service information kiosks on the Mall, near the White House, next to the Vietnam Veterans Memorial, and at several other locations throughout the city, can provide helpful information.
- Dial-A-Park ☎ 202/619–7275 is a recording of events at Park Service attractions in and around Washington.
- Dial-A-Museum ☎ 202/357–2020 is a recording of exhibits and special offerings at Smithsonian Institution museums.

Libraries
- Washington has some two dozen libraries.
- Martin Luther King, Jr. Memorial branch is the main one ✉ 901 G Street NW. You can find information on Washington's history on their Washingtoniana section. Other branches include:
- Georgetown ✉ Wisconsin Avenue and R Street NW ☎ 202/282–0220
- Cleveland Park ✉ Connecticut Avenue and Macomb Street NW ☎ 202/282–3080
- Southeast ✉ 7th and D Streets SE ☎ 202/698–3377
- West End ✉ 24th and L Streets NW ☎ 202/724–8707.

State Regulations
- You must be 21 years old to drink alcohol in Washington, and you may also be required to produce proof of age.

PUBLIC TRANSPORTATION
- The subway (Metro) and bus (Metrobus) systems are run by the Washington Metropolitan Area Transit Authority (WMATA).
- Maps of the Metro system and some bus schedules are available

in all Metro stations or at WMATA headquarters ✉ **600 5th Street NW**

- For general information or a copy of *Getting There by Metro*, a helpful brochure, call ☎ **202/637–7000** 🕐 **Mon–Fri 6AM–10:30PM; Sat, Sun 8AM–10:30PM**
- Consumer assistance ☎ **202/637–1328** Transit police ☎ **202/962–2121**

The Metro

- The city's subway system is one of the cleanest and safest in the country.
- Trains run every few minutes 🕐 **Mon–Thu 5:30AM–midnight; Fri 5:30AM–1AM; Sat 8AM–1AM; Sun 8AM–midnight**
- The basic fare ($1.15) goes up based on how far you are going and the time of day you are riding (fares are higher during rush hours, 5:30–9:30AM and 3–8PM). Maps in stations tell you both the rush hour fare and regular fare to any destination station.
- You need a farecard to ride the Metro, both to enter and to exit. Farecard machines, located in the stations, take coins and $1, $5, $10, and $20 bills (the most change the machine will give you is about $5, so don't use a large bill if you are buying a low-value card).
- Insert your farecard into the slot on the side of the turnstile. Retrieve it once the gate opens as you will need it to exit. On exiting, insert the farecard into the turnstile. If your card is for the exact fare the gate will open and you can exit; if your card still has some money on it, it will again pop out the top of the turnstile. A red "STOP" light means you need more money on your card to leave the station and must go the Addfare machine; insert your card and the machine

will tell you how much additional fare is owed; pay that fare and return to the exit turnstile.

- The farecards are reusable until the card has a value of less than $1.15. Then, should you need another farecard, your old card can be used as cash in the farecard machine by putting it in the "Used Farecard Trade-In" slot.
- A $5 one-day pass is available for unlimited trips on weekends, holidays or after 9:30AM weekdays. These passes are available at Metro Sales Outlets, including the Metro Center station and some hotels, banks, and grocery stores.
- If you plan to transfer to a bus upon leaving the Metro, get a transfer (before boarding your train) from the dispenser located next to the escalator that goes down to the train level.

Buses

- The bus system covers a much wider area than the Metro.
- The fare within the city is $1.15.
- Free bus-to-bus transfers are available from the driver and are good for about 2 hours at designated Metrobus transfer points.

Taxis

- Taxi fares are based on a zone system. Maps showing the zones are displayed in all cabs but even so it is still difficult to know when you are in which zone.
- The base fare for one passenger within a zone is $4, with a $1.50 charge for each extra passenger and a $1 surcharge Mon–Fri 4–6:30PM.
- If you think that you have been overcharged, ask for the driver's name and cab number

and then threaten to call the D.C. Taxicab Commission ☎ 202/645–6018 If you think you've been over-charged for a ride from the airport, call ☎ 202/331–1671

DRIVING & CAR RENTAL

Driving

- The wearing of seat belts is mandatory for the driver and front seat passenger in Washington, Maryland and Virginia.
- Driving in the city is for the patient only; its well-known gridlock is often worsened by building work.
- Although "right turn on red" is permitted, most downtown intersections have signs for-bidding it from 7AM– 7PM or banning it outright. Virginia also allows "left turn on red" when turning into a one-way street from another one-way street.
- The speed limit in Washington is 25 miles per hour unless otherwise stated.
- Parking is a problem in Washing-ton, as the public parking garages fill up quickly with local workers' cars; you might prefer to use public transportation. If you park on city streets, check the signs to make sure it is permitted: green and white signs show when parking is allowed; red and white signs when it is not. Parking on most main streets is not permitted during rush hours, and if you park illegally your car is likely to get towed. If it does, call ☎ 202/727–5000 to find out where it is and how to get it back.

Car rental

- Alamo ☎ 800/327–9633
- Avis ☎ 800/331–1212; 800/879–2847 in Canada
- Budget ☎ 800/527–0700

- Dollar ☎ 800/800–4000
- Hertz ☎ 800/654–3131
- National ☎ 800/227–7368.

MEDIA & COMMUNICATIONS

Newspapers & magazines

- Washington has two major daily newspapers, *The Washington Post* and *The Washington Times*.
- In addition, various neighborhood weekly newspapers serve Capitol Hill, Georgetown, Adams-Morgan and other areas.
- The *City Paper*, a free weekly with an emphasis on entertainment, is available from newspaper boxes around town and at many restaurants, clubs and other outlets.
- The *Washington Blade*, a free weekly aimed at gays and lesbians, is available at many restaurants, bars and stores, especially in the Dupont Circle, Adams-Morgan, and Capitol Hill areas, or at Lambda Rising ✉ 1625 Connecticut Avenue NW ☎ 202/462–6969 or Lammas ✉ 1607 17th Street NW ☎ 202/775–8218
- *Washingtonian*, a monthly magazine, has a calendar of events, dining information, and articles about the city and its prominent people.
- *Where/Washington*, a monthly magazine listing popular things to do, is free at most hotels.
- Other national newspapers are available at newspaper stands.

Television

- The main TV stations are all available: WRC/NBC on Channel 4; WTTG/Fox on Channel 5; WJLA/ABC on Channel 7; WUSA/CBS on Channel 9, and WETA/PBS on Channel 26. Local stations include W28BY IND (public affairs coverage) on Channel 28, and WHUT PBS, operated by Howard University, on Channel 32. Cable channels vary.

Radio
- FM 88.5: WAMU for news, talk and bluegrass music; 89.3 WPFW for jazz, talk and news; 90.1: WCSP for coverage of Congress and public affairs; 90.9 WETA for classical music, news and talk; 96.3: WHUR for adult urban contemporary; 98.7: WMZQ for country music; 103.5: WGMS for classical music, and 106.7: WJFK for talk and Howard Stern.
- AM 630: WMAL for news, and talk; 980: WTEM for sport; 1260: WGAY for easy listening; 1450: WOL for local talk, and 1500: WTOP for news and sport.

Mail
- The National Postal Museum ✉ Massachusetts Avenue and North Capitol Street NE, next door to Union Station, is a working post office.
- Other branches include: Farragut ✉ 1800 M Street NW ☎ 202/523–2506 Georgetown ✉ 1215 31st Street NW ☎ 202/523–2405 L'Enfant Plaza ✉ 458 L'Enfant Plaza SW ☎ 202/523–2013 Washington Square ✉ 1050 Connecticut Avenue NW ☎ 202/523–2631.

EMERGENCIES

Sensible precautions
- Washington is as safe as any large city. Crime is mainly concentrated far from the downtown and tourist areas, places you are unlikely to visit.
- At night, use the same precautions you would use in any city: on quiet streets, always be

aware of what's going on around you; walk with someone rather than alone; use taxis in less populous areas.

Lost property
- Metro or Metrobus ☎ 202/962–1195
- Smithsonian museums: ☎ 202/357–2700
- Other lost articles: check with the police at ☎ 202/727–1010.

Medical treatment
- The hospital closest to downtown is George Washington University Hospital ✉ 901 23rd Street NW ☎ 202/715–4911, emergencies only.
- 1–800–DOCTORS ☎ 800/362–8677 is a referral service that locates doctors, dentists and urgent-care clinics in the greater Washington area.
- The D.C. Dental Society ☎ 202/547–7615 operates a referral line Mon–Fri 8–4.

Medicines
- CVS operates 24-hour pharmacies ✉ 14th Street and at Thomas Circle NW ☎ 202/ 628–0720 and ✉ 7 Dupont Circle NW ☎ 202/785–1466.

Embassies & Consulates
- Germany ✉ 4645 Reservoir Road NW ☎ 202/298–4000 (consulate ☎ 202/298–4393).
- Ireland ✉ 2234 Massachusetts Avenue NW ☎ 202/462–3939
- Italy ✉ 1601 Fuller Street NW ☎ 202/328–5500 (consulate ☎ 202/328–5555).
- Netherlands ✉ 4200 Linnean Avenue NW ☎ 202/244–5300
- Spain ✉ 2375 Pennsylvania Avenue NW ☎ 202/452–0100 (consulate ☎ 202/728–2330).
- United Kingdom ✉ 3100 Massachusetts Avenue NW ☎ 202/588–6500 (consulate ☎ 202/588–7800).

INDEX

Citypack
Washington, D.C.

Time inevitably brings changes, so always confirm prices, travel facts, and other perishable information when it matters. Although Fodor's cannot accept responsibility for errors, you can use this guide in the confidence that we have taken every care to ensure its accuracy.

Copyright   © Automobile Association Developments Limited 1996, 1997, 2000
Maps copyright   © Automobile Association Developments Limited 1996, 1997, 2000
Fold-out map: © RV Reise- und Verkehrsverlag Munich · Stuttgart
                 © Cartography: GeoData

Published in the United States by Fodor's Travel Publications
Published in the United Kingdom by AA Publishing

Fodor's is a registered trademark of Random House, Inc.

ISBN 0–679–00662–1
Third Edition

FODOR'S CITYPACK WASHINGTON, D.C.

AUTHORS *Mary Case and Bruce Walker*
CARTOGRAPHY *Automobile Association Developments Limited*
            RV Reise- und Verkehrsverlag
COVER DESIGN *Tigist Getachew, Fabrizio La Rocca*

THIRD EDITION REVISED BY *Mary Case and Bruce Walker*
REVIEWER *Gerry Wingenbach* INDEXER *Marie Lorimer*
THIRD EDITION UPDATED BY *PITKIN UNICHROME LTD*.

Acknowledgments

The Automobile Association would like to thank the following photographers, libraries, and associations for their assistance in the preparation of this book: Bridgeman Art Library, Peacock Room by James McNeill Whistler, 1876–7, Freer Gallery, Smithsonian Institute, Washington U.S.A. 36a; M. Gostelow 7, 57; Mary Evans Picture Library 36b; The Phillips Collection 27; Pictures Colour Library Ltd 13a; Spectrum Colour Library 13b, 41b. All remaining photographs were taken by Ethel Davies and are held in the Association's own library (AA Photo Library).

Special sales

Fodor's Travel Publications are available at special discounts for bulk purchases (100 copies or more) for sales promotions or premiums. Special editions, including personalized covers, excerpts of existing guides, and corporate imprints, can be created in large quantities for special needs. For more information, contact your local bookseller or write to Special Markets, Fodor's Travel Publications, 280 Park Avenue, New York, NY 10017. Inquiries from Canada should be directed to your local Canadian bookseller or sent to Random House of Canada, Ltd., Marketing Department, 2775 Matheson Boulevard East, Mississauga, Ontario L4W 4P7.

Color separation by Daylight Colour Art Pte Ltd, Singapore
Manufactured by Dai Nippon Printing Co. (Hong Kong) Ltd
10 9 8 7 6 5 4 3 2 1

Titles in the Citypack series

- Amsterdam ● Atlanta ● Barcelona ● Berlin ● Beijing ● Boston ●
- Brussels & Bruges ● Chicago ● Dublin ● Florence ● Hong Kong ● London ●
- Los Angeles ● Madrid ● Miami ● Montreal ● New York ● Paris ● Prague ●
- Rome ● San Francisco ● Seattle ● Shanghai ● Sydney ● Tokyo ● Toronto ● Venice
- Vienna ● Washington, D.C. ●